Wat's Dyke Way Heritage Trail

On Wat's Dyke Way, beside the River Dee at Erbistock

Wat's Dyke Way
Heritage Trail

A 61-mile linear trail plus four circular walks

Pete Lewis

Published by Alyn Books

ISBN: 978-0-9559625-0-9

With thanks to:

Wat's Dyke Way Association Committee members: Ron Williams, Medwyn Roberts, Jim Irvine, Val Walker Jones, Jean Catherall, Jane Ing, Arthur Harris and Dave Martin, former Secretary, Sue Tierney, and the late Dave Fuge, former Treasurer

Officers from the three County Councils: Jon Hill and Kevin Lewis, Flintshire County Council; John Marchant and Dave Smith; Wrexham County Borough Council; Andrew Mallender and Karen Wilson, Shropshire County Council

Ian Bapty, formerly of the Clwyd Powys Archaeological Trust.
Adrian Barksby of the Beaufort Park Hotel
Ros Booty formerly of Groundwork Wrexham and Flintshire

Route checkers:
Cathy Clapp, Clive Menzies, John Roberts, Tony Shorter, Alice Clisby, Huw Thomas, Jackie Lewis and Sarah Brennan

Trail concept and development by the Wat's Dyke Way Association
Research, writing and photography by Pete Lewis
Additional photography by Lorna Jenner, Carl Rogers & Tony Bowerman
Heron and dragonfly images © Simon Booth Photography 2008
Maps by William Smuts

Printed and published in Wales by Gomer Press Ltd., Llandysul, Ceredigion.

British Library Cataloguing-in-publication data.
A catalogue is available for this book from the British Library.
Whilst every effort has been made to ensure that the information in this book is correct, the author or the publisher can accept no responsibility for errors, loss or injury however caused.

Maps based upon out of copyright Ordnance Survey mapping.

Contents

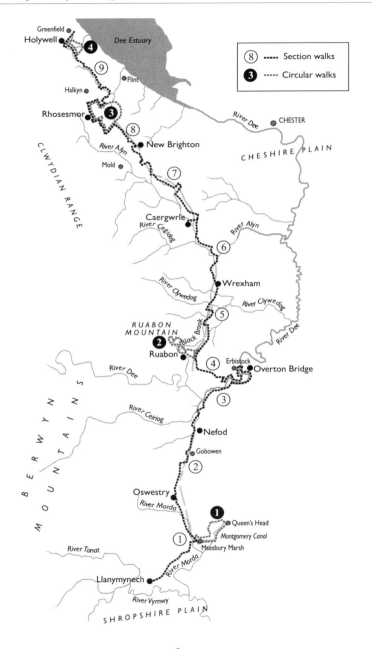

Introduction

Wat's Dyke Way Heritage Trail is an exciting new 61 mile (99km) walk through the border country between England and North Wales. It is based on the route of Wat's Dyke, a major earthwork that is thought to date from the Dark Ages. It crosses three counties, running from the Shropshire village of Llanymynech on the English and Welsh Border, through Wrexham and ending near the Dee Estuary, at Holywell in Flintshire.

The borderlands of north-east Wales have always been a frontier zone, lying between the Cheshire Plain to the east and the Clwydian Range and Berwyns to the west. The westerly edge of the lowlands was a territorial limit for many generations of armies marching from the east into the Welsh heartland. The borderland is known as, 'The Marches', from the Anglo-Saxon word 'mearc', which simply means boundary. The area was a buffer zone between the Romans and the Britons, later contested by the Welsh rulers of Gwynedd and Powys, by Anglo-Saxons, by the forces of Norman barons, Welsh princes and English monarchs, and later, by the Civil War armies of King and Parliament.

Even before the time of Wat's Dyke, the area was scattered with earthwork defences, often sited to reinforce existing natural strong points. The earliest are the Iron Age hillforts on isolated hilltops and promontories along the route and, in the distance, along the Clwydian Range. These impressive prehistoric strongholds may date from 2500 years ago and some continued in use up to, and even after, the Roman conquests of AD 47-78. The route passes several of these hillforts. It is debatable whether they were incorporated as defensive structures within Wat's Dyke but they clearly provided good vantage points to view the land to the west.

Erdigg

The frontier dykes of Wat and Offa were created within this borderland. These great earthworks were a physical manifestation of the border across which numerous generations of Welsh and English traded, intermarried and fought. Offa's Dyke defends the higher ground to the west whilst Wat's Dyke occupies the lowlands. The documented history from this time gives only a limited insight into the political and strategic influences that led to their construction but they remain amongst the most impressive structures of their day.

Whilst the hillforts, dykes and castles reflect the periods of violence and oppression there were also periods of peace and prosperity, reflected in the number of fine churches and elegant country houses. The fertile lowlands were highly prized agriculturally, growing crops and fattening livestock, and several thriving market towns developed.

The minerals in the underlying bedrock also brought wealth to the area. The technological advances of the industrial revolution enabled extraction on a largescale and numerous brickworks, ironworks, quarries, lead mines and collieries were opened. Water power was harnessed at Greenfield Valley to drive cotton and wire mills, and the raw materials and finished products were easily transported via the ports on the nearby Dee Estuary.

As you walk Wat's Dyke Way you will find many reminders not only of the turbulent history of these borderlands but its rich industrial and cultural heritage too.

The History of Wat's Dyke

Wat's Dyke is a linear earthwork, which until recent times has been a neglected landmark, overshadowed by its better-known neighbour Offa's Dyke. Even so, it is still one of the largest archaeological monuments in Britain with approximately 52% of its length listed as a scheduled monument.

Lower Cotton Mill, Greenfield Valley

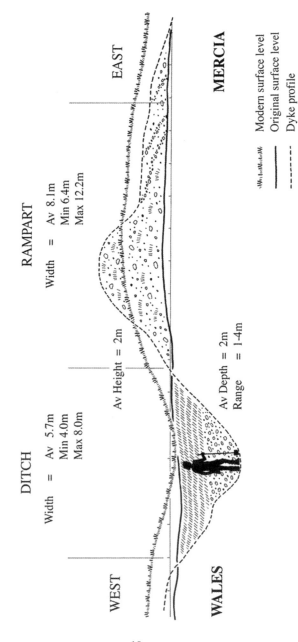

WAT'S DYKE PROFILE

WEST

DITCH

Width = Av 5.7m
Min 4.0m
Max 8.0m

RAMPART

Width = Av 8.1m
Min 6.4m
Max 12.2m

EAST

Av Height = 2m

Av Depth = 2m
Range = 1-4m

WALES

MERCIA

Modern surface level
Original surface level
Dyke profile

It was probably built in the Dark Ages, sometime between 1200 and 1600 years ago, but there is a tantalising lack of real data to pinpoint this more accurately. The Dark Ages are a fascinating, yet frustrating period in the history of the Welsh borderlands; fascinating because it was during this time that the subtle balance between English and Welsh culture developed and also when many places acquired the Anglo-Saxon names by which we now know them; but frustrating because of the absence of firm evidence, either documentary or archaeological, with which to build up a clear picture. Historical accounts of the period are sketchy and therefore often misleading.

What we can say with certainty from the current remains is that the dyke consisted of an earth bank and a ditch. The bank was a little over 8 metres wide at the base on average. Today, it stands about 2 metres high in places but would have originally

A well-preserved section of Wat's Dyke, near Penyffordd

been somewhat higher. It had a turf facing and was mainly composed of soil strengthened with turf layers. The ditch also varied in size but, on average, was 5.7 metres wide and just over 2 metres deep.

Construction of the dyke was no mean undertaking. At 40 miles (65 km) in length, a rough calculation determines that about 500,000m3 of soil and turf was removed from the ditch and subsequently added to the bank. Allowing an average of twenty minutes to excavate a cubic metre of soil and to pile it up in a structured bank, this would give a total of 166,666 man-hours or about 20,000 man-days to build the dyke. One hundred men could have built it in approximately one year!

The deep ditch was always on the west (the Welsh) side, which suggests that it was built by the Mercians against the Welsh. There is speculation about the purpose of the dyke. Some have described it as a frontier, a boundary rampart,

The bank of Wat's Dyke, near Sychdyn

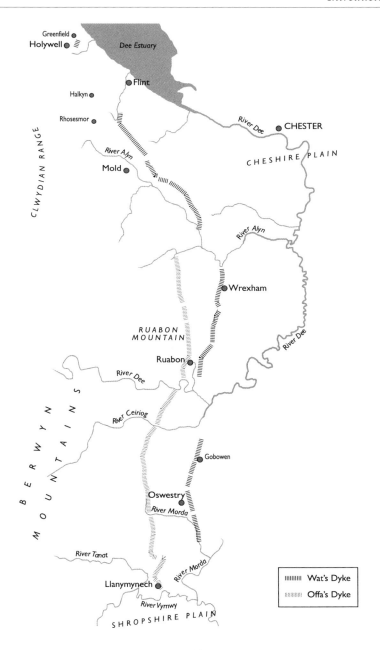

rather than a line of defence. It was probably not built as a defence against a large army but perhaps would have been effective against small groups of raiders whose attacks made agriculture very difficult along the Mercian border. Current opinion suggests that it was a single, almost continuous earthwork, skilfully designed to take advantage of the available natural west-facing features in order to protect the productive agricultural land to the east, just below the foothills of the Welsh uplands.

The start of the southern end of the dyke is difficult to locate precisely but is now thought to have been in marshland south of Oswestry, near Maesbury Mill. This is further south than archaeologists originally believed. It has been suggested that a built boundary wasn't needed further south than this as the River Severn and its northern tributaries provided a natural physical boundary along the border beyond here.

From here, the line of Wat's Dyke can be traced through Oswestry and then continues towards Wrexham, crossing the River Dee near Ruabon. From Wrexham it follows the north and east side of the Alyn Valley, skirts Mold, then turns to run parallel with the Dee Estuary before ending just below the Basingwerk Abbey at Holywell.

From the air the dyke clearly shows as a linear feature, which runs almost north/south along the border area between England and Wales. On the ground it is sometimes more difficult to see but visible remnants can still be found along its length. Inevitably much of it, has been obscured or destroyed by modern building and, visually, the remaining dyke can be disappointing. It often looks much like any other field boundary, a high standing line of hedge with its ditch mostly invisible, long filled or ploughed out. Sometimes it is nothing more than a crop mark. However, there are several sections on the walk where the bank and ditch are far clearer, including near Ruabon, Caergwrle, Penyffordd, Erddig and Sychdyn.

Relationship with Offa's Dyke

The relationship between the two borderland earthworks has long been a puzzle. Offa's Dyke is about 80 miles long and continues south to the Herefordshire Plain but runs close to Wat's Dyke in the north. They were frequently linked together in early writings and often confused. Whilst the name of Offa's Dyke links with a specific period in time, Wat's Dyke remains more of an enigma as it cannot be linked to a specific ruler and the documented and archaeological evidence can be interpreted in several ways.

The earliest reference to the dykes may be Churchyard's Worthines of Wales (1587).

"Within two myles, there is a famous thing,
Cal'de Offae's dyke, that reacheth farre in length,
All kind of ware the Danes might thether bring,
It was free ground, and cal'de the Britaine's strength.
Wat's dyke likewise, about the same was set,
Betweene which two, both Danes and Britaine's met
And trafficke still, but passing bounds by sleight,
The one did take the other pris'ner streight."

Well-known 18th century travel writer, Thomas Pennant, recognised the importance of Wat's Dyke and commented on the frequent confusion.

"A great dike and foss, called Wat's is little known; notwithstanding it is equal in depth, though not in extent, to that of Offa.......... It is so often confounded with Offa's ditch, which attends the former at unequal distances, from five hundred yards to three miles, till the latter is totally lost".

From Oswestry to south of Mold the two earthworks run almost parallel, with Offa's Dyke to the west on higher ground and Wat's Dyke to the east across mostly low-lying agricultural land. In some areas, they stand no more than 1.1 km (1,200 yards) from each other! Wat's Dyke is far shorter but is considered to be better built and better sited. Both have deep west-facing ditches and represented similar military or political demarcation lines. The engineering and design of both dykes is also similar and both appear to be the work of Mercian dyke builders, showing clear planning and organisation. There are small design differences which suggests different architects or foremen were controlling the work but these differences are not great enough to suggest a marked difference in date between them.

Wat's Dyke appears to be a more reasonable frontier against the Welsh than Offa's Dyke, as it would have been much easier to hold. It is not clear why two similar dykes were built in such close proximity.

Beyond Mold the route of Offa's Dyke is unclear, whereas Wat's Dyke is well-defined. It is possible that the two ran together along this final section to the coast. This may explain the frequent name confusions along this section of Wat's Dyke as there are several farmhouses and place names with 'Offa' in their names.

When was it built?

There is very little real evidence on the ground and there are divergent theories on the actual date of construction. Most archaeologists think that Wat's Dyke was built earlier than Offa's Dyke, as it lies to the east. It may be the first formal boundary dividing the Anglo-Saxon kingdom of Mercia (centred on what is now the Midlands) and the Welsh heartland to the west. During the reign of the powerful King Offa (757-796) the Mercians conducted fierce campaigns against the Welsh and penetrated further west. Offa's Dyke was contructed during this period, probably to form a boundary edging the newly won, but still disputed, territory.

Offa's Dyke has been dated quite accurately and the similarity in building styles between the two dykes suggests that Wat's Dyke is from a similar period. However, it is improbable that they were both built by Offa as the enormous task of building two earthworks would not have been realistic or necessary. It is likely to have been built by one of the preceding rulers. It is most frequently attributed to Æthelbald, Offa's immediate predecessor, who ruled the whole of Mercia. Others believe it may have been built slightly earlier to protect Cheshire to the north-west, which had been aquired by the Mercians in the middle of the 7th century.

Others argue that Wat's Dyke was built after Offa's Dyke, as it is better built and sited. However, the king who followed Offa was also an active fighter who is known to have been

Illustration: Anne Robinson

Artist's impression of digging Wat's Dyke

campaigning west of Offa's Dyke and so was unlikely to build a boundary to the east. Thereafter Mercia rapidly declined, following its conquest by the West Saxons in 829, rendering massive building projects all but impossible.

One relatively recent find of charcoal below the bank of Wat's Dyke at Maes-y-Clawdd, near Oswestry, has been radiocarbon dated to around AD 446. This could bring the date of the dyke construction 300 years earlier than was previously thought. Shropshire Archaeologists concluded that the dyke may be contemporary with the Wiltshire Wansdyke rather than with the Offa's Dyke, making it Post-Roman rather than Mercian. However, this date is based on the age of the burned wood not the actual dyke itself. The wood may have been from a recently felled tree or it may have been old timber. All that can be concluded for certain is that the dyke is defintely older than the timber, ie built after AD446, but it could be several centuries older!

Who was Wat?

The name of the dyke is another enigma! Once again there are numerous theories but no clear evidence! Wat is an Old English personal name but the earliest records of the dyke use the name Wada or variations on it. This suggests that the current name may not be as old as the dyke itself. Wada occurs as a saga hero in Old English folklore and as a mythical creature in Germanic folklore. Several earlier dykes including Grim's Ditches and Wansdyke are named after mythological beings rather than historical personages so this is a real possibility.

It is unlikely to be named after a member of the Mercian Royal dynasty as there were no Wadas. The only Wat recorded was King of the South Saxons in 692 but he was not known to be active in North Wales.

Wat may have been a military leader commissioned to design and build a defensive feature along the border, or an important local dignitary.

Others have suggested that there could be a link with Watling Street, the Roman road connecting the channel ports with Chester. Alternatively the word could mean "wet" or "rough", which would certainly suit this earthwork, as it follows a number of the river valleys!

The truth is we may never know for certain who Wat was or where the name comes from. Equally, we may never fully understand the historical context that produced the dyke but that does not diminish its place as an intriguing and important feature in the landscape of north-east Wales.

The Walk Route

It is a predominatly lowland walk but it does include some slightly higher ground, as the dyke itself took advantage of natural land features, so there are often excellent views across into Wales.

The terrain is varied from canal towpaths and quiet riversides in the south to small wooded valleys and country lanes in the north. It crosses rolling farmland grazed with sheep and cattle, grand parkland of big estates like Erddig and Wynnstay, and numerous picturesque villages and hamlets such as Llanymynech with its lime-working heritage, canal-side Maesbury Marsh, Caergwrle with its Welsh castle and packhorse bridge, riverside Erbistock, and Ruabon with its brick and tile -making links.

It also passes through the historic towns of Oswestry, Wrexham and Holywell. The walking in these sections is

Along the Montgomery canal, near Maesbury Marsh

The Guildhall, Oswestry

inevitably more urban, but the guide draws out the rich history of each town which adds to the story of life on the English and Welsh borders.

For wildife lovers there's plenty to see as well. Dragonflies and damselflies hover above the canal and ducks and swans feed in the sluggish waters. Along the faster flowing rivers and streams herons hunt for fish and slender grey wagtails flit above the water catching flying insects. You may even be lucky enough to glimpse a kingfisher.

The damp woodlands, with luxuriant ferns and mosses, are carpeted with spring flowers such as bluebells, violets, primroses and pungent wild garlic. In summer honeysuckle and dog-rose tumble over the thick hedgerows and the grassy verges are full of wildlfowers such as harebells, ox-eye daisies and red campion. The autumn colours are wonderful and the feast of berries and nuts sustains numerous birds, mice and voles through the winter.

Using this Guide

Each walk is illustrated with a map and detailed route directiosn to enable you to find and follow the routes. The Wat's Dyke waymarker has been used at key junctions but the route is not fully waymarked so always take along the relevant Ordnance Survey Explorer map too. The maps covering the route are 240 Oswestry, 256 Wrexham and Llangollen, 266 Wirral and Chester and 265 Clwydian Range. Familiarising yourself with the map and route before setting off will ensure you are well-prepared.

We have provided interpretive text in italics for each walk, giving glimpses into the history, wildlife and landscape. Additional information is also available at a number of the historic sites along the route.

The linear walk is divided into nine sections. There are also four circular routes along the length of the walk, which give an opportunity to explore some of the surrounding countryside in more depth.

Heron

Always ensure you wear suitable walking shoes and clothing appropriate for the time of the year. The riverside section will be much more difficult to negotiate after heavy rain and extra caution needs to be taken. Many of the sections pass pubs and shops, but check opening hours before you set out. Always take plenty to drink and spare food with you.

Please be sensitive to the needs of local residents and farmers and follow the country code at all times.

- Be safe – plan ahead and follow any signs

- Leave gates and property as you find them

- Protect plants and animals, and take your litter home

- Keep dogs under close control

- Consider other people

If you are taking a dog please clear up after them and ensure that they are kept under close control at all times, particularly near livestock. Take particular care during the lambing and calving season. Cows are very protective of their calves and can chase dogs.

There are numerous stiles on some sections that may give difficulty for the elderly. The text gives a clear indication of the number of stiles in each section to help you choose your route.

Further information and feedback

The Wat's Dyke Way web site (www.watsdykeway.org) provides information on accommodation and any route changes or blockages. The website also includes a message board for giving feedback about the route. If you have any problems with route finding or have any additional information please use the message board to inform other walkers and to enable us to amend the directions at the next reprint. If you encounter any blockages on rights of way along the route please also contact the relevant rights of way department.

Shropshire: tel: 01743 255061
e-mail: countryside.access@shropshire.gov.uk
Wrexham: tel: 01978 297060
e-mail: rightsofway@wrexham.gov.uk
Flintshire: tel: 01352 704622
e-mail: rightsofway@flintshire.gov.uk

For additional walks in each county please contact:

www.wrexham.gov.uk/countryside

www.flintshire.gov.uk/countryside

www.shropshire.gov.uk/countryside.nsf

www.shropshirewalking.co.uk

Public Transport

The walk is divided into 9 linear sections. Some sections can be easily accessed via public transport but others are more difficult and ideally require two cars. The public transport options for the sections between Moreton and Ruabon were particularly limited. Details of the bus and trains at time of writing are given at the beginning of each walk but services frequently change so please check with the service provider when planning your route.

For all bus and train information
Traveline 0871 200 22 33

For up to date local bus timetable information contact;
Flintshire BusLine on 01352 704035 or www.flintshire.gov.uk

Wrexham BusLine on 01978 266166 or
www.wrexham.gov.uk/bus or www.wrecsam.gov.uk/bws

Shropshire Traveline on 08712002233 or
www.shropshire.gov.uk

Train Information
The National Rail Enquires 08457 484950

The Development of Wat's Dyke Way

The original idea for a long-distance walking trail based on Wat's Dyke was formulated by Medwyn Roberts in the late 1990s. As both a keen walker and Town Centre Manager for Holywell that lies at the northern end of the dyke, he recognised the leisure value and the economic benefits such a path could bring for towns and villages along the route. In 2001 the Wat's Dyke Association was established to develop he route. It was chaired by Ron Williams, North Wales Area Secretary of Ramblers' Association, who had the foresight to see the potential of developing the route as a heritage trail, capitailising on its fascinating borderland history and superb industrail archaeology. Members of the Wat's Dyke Association, in partnership with officers from Flintshire County Council, Wrexham County Borough Council and Shropshire County Council, mapped out the route and negotiated access issues. Their work culminated in the official opening of the trail and the publication of this guidebook in summer 2008.

They also ran a competition for schools along the route to design a Wat's Dyke waymarker. The winning entry was designed by Conor Kendrick from St Mary's Church in Wales Primary School, Ruabon. His design illustrates the dyke and the two holy wells along the route that are both dedicated to St Winefride!

The Welsh language

The changing ownership of the land is also reflected in the place names. We find both English derived place names in what is now Wales and Welsh derived names in what is now England. In the north the land to the east of the dyke contains a high proportion of Old English place names (albeit, often with a later Welsh disguise). The area west of the dyke, by contrast, is much more 'Welsh' in terms of place names. In the south the Welsh and English place names intermix reflecting the frequently changing ownership of the land, as well as trading between the different communities.

This following glossary gives a useful insight into the meanings of many of the common components of Welsh place names. The origins of names encountered along the route are explained in more detail in each chapter.

Glossary of Welsh names

Abaty	abbey	Hafod	summer dwelling
Afon	river	Hen	old
Allt	hillside	Isaf	lower
Bach/fach	little/ small	Llan	church
Bryn	hill, eminence	Llyn	lake
Cae	field, enclosure	Llys	hall or court
Caer	fort	Lôn	lane
Canol	middle	Maen	stone
Capel	chapel	Maes	meadow
Carn, Carnedd	heap of stones	Mor	sea
Carreg	crag or stone	Mynach	monk
Castell	castle or fortress	Mynydd	mountain
Cefn	ridge	Newydd	new
Clwyd	gate	Ogof	cave
Coch/Goch	red	Pant	hollow
Coed	wood	Parc	park
Cors	bog or swamp	Pen	head or point
Craig	crag	Penrhyn	promontory
Croes/Groes	cross	Pentre	village
Cwm	coombe	Pistyll	waterfall
Dinas	city/fortress	Plas	house
Du/Ddu	black	Pont	bridge
Dyffryn	valley	Porth	port
Eglwys	church	Pwll	pool
Eryri	highland	Rhos	moorland
Esgair	ridge	Rhyd	ford
Faes	meadow	Sarn	causeway
Fawr/Mawr	large	Tomen	mound
Felin	mill	Tref	town
Ffordd	road	Twll	cavern
Ffynnon	well or fountain	Twr	tower
Foel/Moel	round or bare hill	Ty	house
Gaer	camp	Tyddyn	farmstead
Galt	slope	Uchaf	upper
Glas	blue-green	Waun	moorland
Glyn	deep valley	Wen	white
Gors	swamp	Wern/Gwern	alder swamp
Grach	scabby	Y, Yr	the
Gwyn	white	Yn	in

27

Llanymynech - Oswestry

Distance: 12.5 km (7.8 miles)
Time: 4.0 – 4.5hrs

From Llanymynech the route follows the towpath of the Montgomery Canal to Maesbury Marsh then crosses farmland to the historic town of Oswestry.

Parking: Small car park at the Llanymynech Heritage Area just off the A483 before the canal bridge and public car park behind The Dolphin pub.
Grid ref: SJ 267211; **Map:** OS Explorer 240.
Facilities: Pubs and shop in Llanymynech; cafe/shop (Canal Central) and pub in Maesbury Marsh; all facilities in Oswestry
Public Transport: No.71, 71A & 445 buses, Welshpool-Oswestry.

The Walk
The first written record of Llanemenych dates from 1254. The name was thought to mean 'Place of the Miners' but is probably a derivation from Welsh; Llan = church or village y = of the and mynach = monk.

The village nestles below limestone Llanymynech Hill. Limestone is rich in minerals and copper, silver, zinc and lead were all mined here, some as far back as the Bronze Age. There is evidence that the Romans were also attracted by the mineral wealth as a hoard of Roman coins were found by local schoolboys in a cave in 1965. However it was the limestone itself that proved the most valuable and it has been

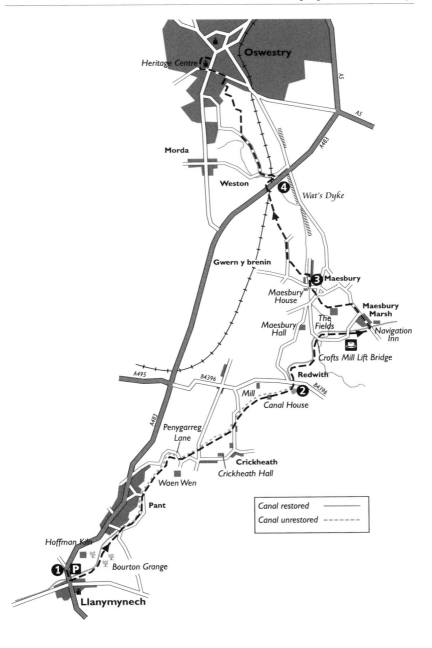

Hoffman kiln chimney, Llanymynech

extensively quarried, particularly in the 18th and 19th centuries. The rock itself was used for building and as a flux in iron smelting. Much was burned in limekilns to produce quicklime that was used to make building mortar and fertiliser. To learn more about the local lime industry detour to explore the Heritage Area.

1. From the Heritage Area car park go back to the busy A483. Beside the road is a sculpture by Anthony Lysycia that represents the area's history and industrial past. Turn left to cross the canal bridge then immediately left down some steps to join the canal towpath.

Llanymynech spans the English/Welsh border and, as the Montgomery Canal passes underneath Llanymynech Bridge, it crosses from England into Wales. This branch of the canal, opened in 1795, was built to serve the local lime industry, transporting the quarried stone and burned lime to market, and bringing coal to fire the limekilns from pits at Trefonen and Morda, near Oswestry. The canal gave a further boost to the already thriving industry as a horse could transport less than 1 ton of limestone by road but could pull a barge loaded with 55 tons!

The railway was opened in 1863. At first it had limited impact on the canal but it eventually took much of the trade away. By the early 20th century, traffic was slight and the canal was only viable as a feeder to the main Shropshire Union system. When a major breach happened below Welsh Frankton locks in 1936 the canal was abandoned.

Turn right and follow the canal towpath past the former Llanymynech Wharf and the tall red brick chimney of the Hoffman limekiln on the opposite side.

The Hoffman kiln was built around 1899 but it was only used until 1914. The ring kiln was fuel efficient as it could be continuously burned but the process was very labour intensive and the work unpleasant and dangerous. The demand for lime reduced when cement replaced lime mortar for building and there was a labour shortage during the First World War so production steadily waned.

Five vertical limekilns, near Llanymynech

Pass a partially collapsed red brick railway bridge. Beyond this the canal becomes silted up but continue following the obvious line of the former track of the canal.

The derelict canal has reverted to nature. In the water-filled sections aquatic plants now thrive, including several rare floating species, such as frogbit and grass-wrack pondweed. The aquatic vegetation provides homes for many damselflies and dragonflies. The aquatic insects, in turn support fish such as bream, roach, pike, carp and tench.

After passing under a brick bridge pass five vertical limekilns on the left.

The limestone was brought down from the quarries to the canal-side via a tramway with a series of inclined planes. Some stone was directly loaded onto barges for transport to the Black Country iron works but much was burned in the limekilns producing quicklime that was used for fertiliser for acidic soils and for making building mortar. Quicklime is very reactive with water and so it would have

Swans nesting

been a challenge for the barge owners to transport it safely along the canal! For this reason much quicklime may have continued to be transported by horse and cart and, later, by rail. Alternatively it may have been hydrated before transport to form slaked lime, which is less reactive with water.

The route continues past a collapsed railway bridge then bears slightly right to follow a bank with a lane on the right. Cross a stile with no footplate then continue along the obvious route over a further stile then under the Pant Bridge. Go ahead for 0.5 km crossing two stiles.

Through Pant the canal ran alongside the Oswestry and Newtown Railway, which later became part of the Cambrian Railways network. Pant means 'hollow' in Welsh, thus linking the village name with it's mining history. Pant is also renowned for having the golf course where Ian Woosnam learnt to play.

Continue to Waen Wen Bridge. Go under the bridge and through the kissing gate immediately after. Continue along the towpath to School House Bridge. Go up the slope to go through a kissing gate, across a lane and on through a small gate opposite.

Crickheath Hall to the right is a 17th century farmhouse made from rough cast bricks with a wooden frame.

Continue alongside the disused canal crossing two stiles then under Crickheath Bridge. Go under the next bridge, beside a white cottage (Canal House) and continue alongside the canal that was being renovated at time of writing.

2. Go under the new red brick bridge (Redwith Bridge) to join the refurbished navigable canal. Continue along the towpath passing a new lift bridge by Moreton Farm then under another bridge to walk past an old wharf and Crofts Mill Lift Bridge.

Montgomery Canal

Gronwen Wharf was the trans-shipment point for the three mile long feeder tramway known as the Gronwen Colliery or Morda Tramway, which ceased operating around 1879. Just before the reaching Croft Mill Lift Bridge there is a private arm of the canal on the left, which was originally built to bring grain from Chester, Ellesmere Port and Liverpool to Maesbury Hall Mill. Today it is used for building and maintaining canal boats. It is thought that the southern-most section of Wat's Dyke begins close to the lift bridge. On the left is a wildlife area, created when the new lift bridge was built in the early 21st century. A pair of swans regularly nests here and are often seen in spring with their cygnets.

Continue along the towpath past Bridge House. For refreshments, go through the gate on the right just before the next bridge and turn right to Canal Central Cafe and Post Office. Otherwise continue along the towpath under the bridge.

From about the mid 19th century the area just before and after Navigation Bridge were industrial wharves with large warehouses. The wharves were piled high with coal, timber, bricks etc, mainly for onward transportation to Oswestry. The warehouse on this side burned down in 1968. A crane survived the fire and is currently being renovated and should be returned to the site.

Go under Navigation Bridge then immediately turn right up the slope and turn right again over the bridge past the Navigation Inn.

The Navigation Inn was a pub before the canal was built although the present name undoubtedly relates to the canal!

Continue along the main Maesbury Road then take the second left onto a track going past 'The Fields'. At the farm buildings, the track goes to the left. Turn right through a gateway, then immediately left at waymarker, along a narrow path around fields, then cross stream and on through wet meadow. Turn half-right to cross over stile into arable field then along left-hand field edge to exit over a stile onto a lane (with care). Cross the lane and over a stile into a small copse. Exit the copse over a stile to go across a field and back onto a lane at a corner by Maesbury House. Turn left towards Gwern y brenin.

Gwern y brenin translates as 'King's Marsh'. The name is reputed to have arisen when King Henry II set up camp in the area in 1163.

3. Continue straight ahead along Ball Lane, ignoring the next turn on the left. A little after the phone box, turn left over a metal footbridge, then turn right over a stile and half-left across the field. Continue under the power lines to cross a stile to the right of the cottage (ignore the stile directly at rear of the house). Go across the next field to cross a stile opposite then turn left and follow the left-hand hedge to cross a stile. Turn right and follow the lane past Gwern-hafod (translates as

Marsh Farm) then left over a stile. Go half-right to cross a stile in the far right corner. Follow the right hand field boundary through a gate then an open gateway. Go half-left to cross a stile in the middle of the opposite boundary. Continue in the same direction across the next field to cross a stile in the far left corner. Cross the corner of the next field and over a stile in left-hand boundary. Then cross a railway track and go over the stile opposite into a small copse. Go through the copse and over a stile onto the busy A483. Cross the road carefully by the island on the left then turn right, back over the railway. Go behind the barrier, over the stream then left over a stile. Continue down the bank to go through a stile/gateway then cross the railway for the third time and go over stile opposite. Go half-right over a footbridge crossing the river then carefully cross another stile straight onto Weston Road (take care).

The Heritage and Tourist Information Centre, Oswestry

4. Turn left then almost immediately turn right over a bridge to follow Weston Lane. Just after Weston Farm turn right through a kissing gate and walk between two hedges. Go past the first kissing gate on the right instead continue on to a further kissing gate. Go through and bear half right to go through another kissing gate then follow the right hand boundary to a kissing gate on the edge of a cemetery. Go left initially between the hedge and chain link fence then right to follow the hedge line to turn left through a kissing gate (ignore kissing gate opposite). Continue behind houses then turn right along Queen's Road then left along Victoria Road, which later becomes Lower Brook Street. At the junction with Church Street cross the road at the traffic lights and continue along Upper Brook Street.

The fabric shop on the corner of Church Street and Upper Brook Street was originally built for Edward Lloyd of Llanforda in 1660 to stable his dog cart (a light four wheeled carriage) and team of dogs while he attended church. It later became the Coach and Dogs Inn then in contrast became a temperance cocoa house in 1882!

Within 50m turn right down a cobbled alleyway leading to the Heritage & Tourist Information Centre, passing through Griddle Gate, which was erected in 1631.

The Heritage & Tourist Information Centre is housed in a 15th century timber-framed grade II listed building on the periphery of the churchyard and is an excellent source of information on the town and surrounding area. The building was originally built in 1407, a few years before Agincourt, and housed the second oldest Grammar School in the country, founded by David Holbache. When the school moved to new premises at the end of Upper Brook Street in 1776, the old building was used first as a workhouse, then as private housing, and later as the Museum of Childhood, before assuming its current role.

Oswestry - Nefod

Distance: 8km (5 miles)
Time: 2.5 - 3hrs

This walk starts in the historic town of Oswestry then passes an Iron Age hillfort and follows some well-preserved sections of Wat's Dyke before finally crossing the Llangollen Canal to reach Nefod.

Parking: Several car parks in Oswestry town centre.
Grid ref: SJ287293; **Map:** OS Explorer 240.
Facilities: All facilities in Oswestry.
Public Transport: BusNo 2, Oswestry Glendrid Roundabout.

The Walk

Oswestry is named after St Oswald, Christian King of Northumbria, who was slain at the Battle of Maserfield by the Mercian King Penda in AD 642. Oswald's body was hung, drawn and quartered and nailed to a tree. Tradition has it that an eagle carried off the remains, but the arm of the saint fell to the ground and water gushed from the spot, which is now called St Oswald's Well. A settlement developed around the church, and later a castle was built on the nearest glacial mound to the church.

Oswestry is only a few miles from the Welsh border and up to 1535 it changed hands several times. Since then it has been an English town, but many of its residents can claim a Welsh background. Oswestry's situation and importance as a market town meant that trade between the two countries flourished here and Welsh is still heard on market days.

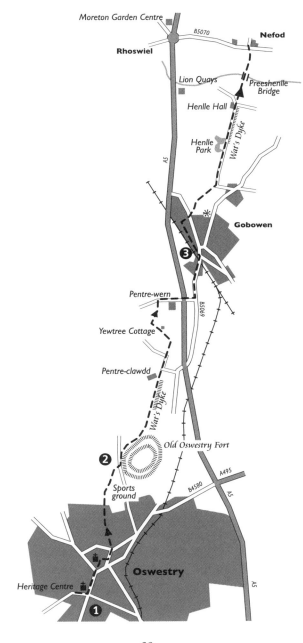

In the Civil War, Oswestry remained loyal to the King but its Royalist forces were defeated by the Parliamentarians. In retribution the castle and town walls were destroyed, but the four town gates on the main roads into town survived and acted as tollgates until the 1780s when they too were demolished.

1. From the Heritage Centre go through the grounds of St. Oswald's Church

Little remains of the original medieval church as it was badly damaged by Parlimentarian troops during the Civil War. Some parts of the 93foot high tower are medieval but the present building largely dates from 1807 when it was rebuilt. A new entrance door was built at the chancel end of the church in 1831 and new pews were installed. The fine church gates, made by Elias Phillips of Pentrepoeth, were erected in 1815 and cost the princely sum of £8.

Turn left onto Church Street. Opposite is the Bell Inn and a little further on is the Wynnstay Arms Hotel.

St Oswald's Church, Oswestry

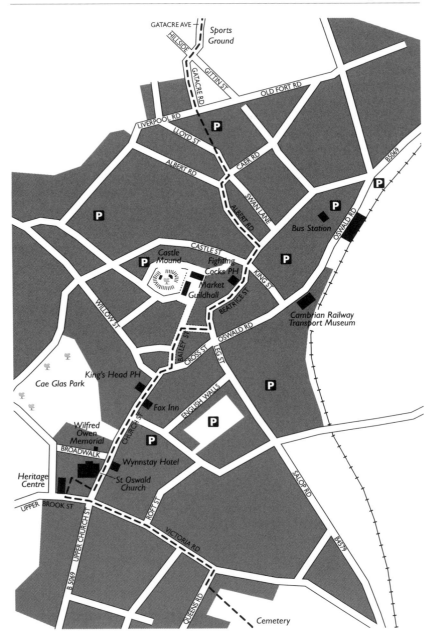

The half-timbered Bell Inn is the oldest established inn in Oswestry, mentioned in parish registers as far back as the 1660s. The Wynnstay Arms was just an ordinary inn until 1800 but was developed to cater for the London to Holyhead coach trade, providing food for the travellers and a change of horses. When Princess Victoria (later Queen) visited Oswestry in 1832 her coach stopped at the Wynnstay. It is said that the crowd waiting to see her was so great that one woman was killed in the crush.

Further on again on the left, behind some impressive wrought iron gates, is the Broad Walk which runs alongside St. Oswald's Church between the site of the old town walls and Church Street. This pleasant tree-lined avenue has a plaque dedicated to Wilfred Owen, the World War 1 poet, who was born in Oswestry in 1893. Wilfred Owen was killed on the 4th November, 1918 a week before the Armistice.

Seventy metres further on the left is the entrance to Cae Glas Park that was originally the gardens of a long demolished mansion. The

Sculpture on Festival Square, near the site of the old livestock market

Memorial Gates at the entrance honours local men who died in the two World Wars.

On the right is the Festival Square, which until 1849, was the site of Oswestry's livestock market.

On the right set into the wall about half way along Church Street, is a white stone pillar with the crest of the Earls of Powis, which marks the location of the New Gate, one of the four original town wall gates.

At the junction of Cross Street and Bailey Street stands Llwyds Mansion, one of Oswestry's best-known buildings. It is an impressive timber framed building with fine window tracery, believed to have been built for John Llwyd of Llanforda in 1604. On the side of the building is the Llwyd family crest of the double-headed eagle.

Cross Willow Street and continue up Bailey Street.

The Guildhall, on the left-hand side of Bailey Head, replaced an older building, which was demolished in 1891. The new Guildhall, which opened in November 1893, housed the council chamber, county court offices and a police station with cells on the ground floor. On the first floor were the courts, robing rooms, grand jury room, a witness' waiting room and a large reading room for the library, which was on the top floor. The Guildhall is now home to Oswestry Archives, housing an impressive collection of documents dating back to the 14th century.

Oswestry market is one of the oldest in the county with a charter dating back to 1407. The Corn Market, or Powis Market as it is now known, is the modern structure directly ahead, built in the 1960s to replace an earlier hall dating from 1869.

The Red Lion pub dates back to the 1660s although, like the Eagle across the square, it has a 19th century frontage. From 1840 to 1843, the Welsh Congregationalists held services in a room over the kitchen on alternate Sundays.

The open ground on Bailey Head was once a place of punishment with stocks and whipping post.

Turn right before the Guildhall to go down Albion Hill then bear left along Beatrice Street.

The gabled Fighting Cocks, despite its name, was never used for cock fighting. These reputedly took place at the George Hotel on Bailey Street, between 1750 and 1800.

Continue down Beatrice Street to reach the Plough Inn on the left.

On the side wall of the pub is a plaque marking the site of the old East or Beatrice Gate. The gate is said to have been named after Beatrice, the wife of Henry IV.

Cross Castle Street after The Plough Inn then turn left up Albert Road opposite the petrol station. At the junction with Castlefields continue ahead then right into Caer Road then first left into Lloyd Street. Bear right through the car park and across Liverpool Road, then continue ahead along Gatacre Road with the allotments on the right. At the junction with Hillside and Gittins Street continue ahead onto Gatacre Avenue. Just before the Sports Ground car park take the footpath on the left. (If this is overgrown continue through the car park to an opening in the left-hand boundary further on). Go through to a kissing gate then half-right across a field to another kissing gate and a lane. To visit Old Oswestry Fort cross the lane and go through the kissing gate opposite.

Old Oswestry (Hen Dinas) is one of the finest examples of an Iron Age hillfort in the Marches, mainly because of its highly elaborate defences. The hill upon which Old Oswestry sits is unusually low for an Iron Age hillfort so it may have been necessary to have more complex ramparts to slow any forces attempting to attack the settlement. Despite its low height, on a clear day there are commanding views from the summit. The fort, which occupies an area of some six hectares, is surrounded by a series of five ramparts and ditches but on the west side the number of ramparts increases to an impressive seven. The western entrance is of great interest to archaeologists as it features a series of deep rectangular hollows that are unique to Old Oswestry. Their purpose is unclear and suggestions vary, from water tanks to quarries or even extra fortifications.

2. Having visited the hillfort return to the lane and turn right. After walking approximately 100m along the lane turn right over a stile by a gate and fingerpost. Initially follow the right-hand boundary then go half-left to cross a stile in the opposite corner. Continue ahead along the right-hand field boundary to a further stile by a gate on right before the field corner. Cross and go half-left to cross stile to the right of Pentre-clawdd House. Go ahead along a tarmac lane, ignoring the turning right, but when the lane turns sharply left by the junction with another track, continue ahead along right-hand field boundary. The route is now following the course of Wat's Dyke, recognisable as a ditch and bank. Before a gate/stile go left to cross a stile hidden in hedge just to the left of Yewtree Cottage. Go right then keep to the left of the cottage, through a hedge, to cross a footbridge and stile. Follow the left-hand field boundary to cross a stile by a large tree in the new fence/hedge line opposite. Continue ahead to cross a stile in the hedge opposite then turn right along the lane. Follow the lane as it crosses over the main A5 and continue to a T-Junction. Turn left along the B5069 into Gobowen.

Gobowen is an old village, with open cast mining recorded as early as 1160. Known as Gobs, it is possible one of these workings could have been owned by a man called Owen, hence the name.

3. Cross the railway track then keep left, past the war memorial to reach a roundabout. Take the first left by the Wesleyan Chapel and almost immediately right into Old Chirk Road. Turn right after the church to reach a crossroads by a school. Continue ahead into School Lane then left through a gate between two hedges past the back of houses to go through a kissing gate. Continue over the footbridge, and straight on up and over a small hill, then past a pond on the left to a kissing gate in the corner of the field. Go through the kissing gate then left up the tarmac lane for 1 km. The clear ditch and bank on the right is the remains of Wat's Dyke. Continue past Henlle Hall on the left to a T-junction. Go ahead along the dirt track to join a fenceline on the left. Follow this, crossing the Llangollen Canal at Preeshenlle Bridge, then cross a stile by a small gate. Continue along the left-hand field boundary, cross a footbridge then turn left up the slope and over a stile. Cross a disused railway track and down the opposite slope to cross over a further stile. Go ahead to the left-hand side of a black corrugated farm building and on through the farmyard to join the B5070.

The next section of Wat's Dyke Way continues along Nefod Lane, across the road to the left.

Oswestry Old Fort, Iron Age hillfort

Nefod - Overton Bridge

Distance: 14.2 km (8.8 miles)
Time: 4.5 - 5hrs

A walk along quiet country lanes, passing the site of a Roman fort, then on through woodland and gently rolling farmland with spectacular views over the Ceiriog Valley towards the Vale of Llangollen and Llantysilio Mountain, finally following the banks of the River Dee past the small hamlet of Erbistock to Overton Bridge.

Parking: Small lay-by at Moors Bank just beyond industrial Estate on B5070.
Grid ref: SJ 312361; **Map:** OS Explorer 240 and 256.
Facilities: Pub in Overton Bridge.
Public Transport: None available at time of writing.

NB Much of this route follows the waymarked Maelor Way, devised by Gordon Emery

The Walk

1. From the lay-by at Moor's Bank cross the road and turn left to walk back along the B5070 towards the roundabout at Rhosweil. Cross the bridge over the stream and turn right down Nefod Lane. Wat's Dyke is immediately to the right along this section. After about 400m the tarmac lane becomes a grassy track. Continue ahead for another 200m then turn right over a stile. Go half-left across the field to cross a further stile, then turn right along Rhyn Lane.

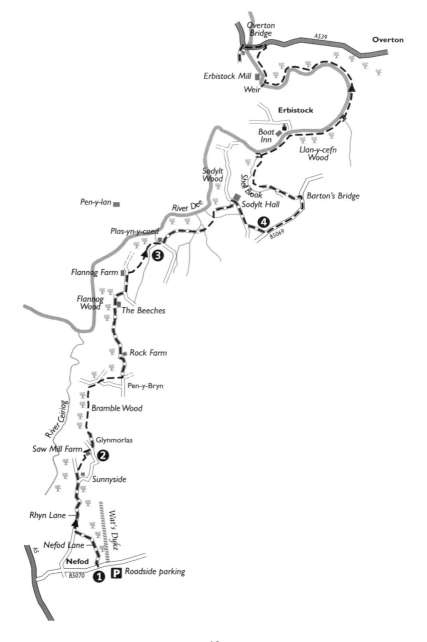

Photographs of crop marking taken during the drought of 1976 produced evidence of a Roman fort to the left on Rhyn Park. Excavations on the site showed two overlapping encampments of different ages. It is believed that the forts predate Chester and were a major strategic base linked to the Roman city of Wroxeter via a march camp at Whittington.

The larger fortress may be related to the initial campaigns of governor Publius Ostorius Scapula against the Iron Age tribe, the Deceangi of North Wales, around AD47. It may also have been used when, in AD60, Suetonius Paullinus attacked North Wales and invaded Anglesey to wipe out the Druids. The large fortress was succeeded by a smaller fort, possibly during the Welsh campaigns of governor Sextus Julius Frontinus circa AD75. It is probable that the base was abandoned when the fortress at Chester was built.

Continue for 700m to pass 'Keeper Cottage' then stay left at the fork. At the entrance to 1 Rhyn Lane cross stile on right and follow the left-hand fence line to cross the next stile. Go half-right descending the slope heading to the left-hand side of Saw Mill Farm. Cross the footbridge over the river before going around the farm then through a gate onto the lane.

This lane was once trodden by miners going to Black Park Colliery near Chirk and was known locally as 'Cat's Walk'.

2. Go right then immediately left uphill on a tarmac lane marked 'Unsuitable for Motor Vehicles', keeping Glenbrook Cottage on the left.

In spring, comfrey grows on the verges, attracting bumblebees and moths. Comfrey is also known as 'boatman's cabbage', due to its profusion and use on canals, and 'knit bone' as its dried and ground root, was used as a plaster. The plant is used in many natural remedies as it contains allantoin, a protein that stimulates cell growth and helps wounds to heal. More recent research has revealed that the plant also contains vitamin B12 and it may be the only vegetable source of this vitamin. Organic gardeners grow the plant as a green manure as its long roots absorb minerals from deep in the soil and it produces an enormous weight of green leaves each year per acre.

Turn left at footpath sign just beyond a house, Woodside, to go around a building and into Bramble Wood. Continue uphill, (do not descend on more obvious track) then branch right to a stile. Cross the stile and continue along the left-hand boundary above the wood, crossing two further stiles. After the second go half-right, keeping well to the left of the farm. Cross a stile and go down a steep slope to the lane and up the steps opposite to cross a stile into a field.

The tithe map of 1838 records the name of this field as Cae ffynon, which is Welsh for Well Field. Welsh and English names can be found all over the Marches. The borders changed so often, even after Wat and Offa had built their Dykes, as the Norman Marcher lords only had their boundaries set on the English side and were free to hold whatever land they could defend and maintain on the Welsh side.

View to Ceiriog Valley and Vale of Llangollen

Go ahead towards the opposite left-hand corner to cross a stile. Turn right and head up the field to go over the next stile. Continue along the right hand field boundary to go over a stile by a gate, which leads to a lane. Turn left and continue along the lane, (good views to the left over the River Ceiriog and along the Vale of Llangollen to Llantysilio Mountain) eventually passing Rock Farm. The tarmac lane stops at the Beeches but continue on the grassy track ahead to eventually reach another tarmac lane then turn left. At the entrance to Flannog Farm, go through a gate on the right then keep to the right of a large tank to cross a stile in the boundary opposite then half- right to go through a gate.

Spring walkers may notice the pink hawthorn just before the gate. The flower colour is a result of a cross between the red midland hawthorn and the more common cream-flowered variety.

To the left, on the opposite side of the river, is a large house, Pen-y–lan (translates as 'top of the church land'). The original house is said to date from 1690 but was remodelled in 1830 resulting in the grand stuccoed and castellated house that remains today.

3. Continue ahead on muddy path, initially along the left-hand fenceline, through a wood to a wooden bridge. Cross the bridge, but do not go through gate ahead, instead bear right up a slope to go through another gate. Follow the left-hand field boundary past Plas-yn-y-coed (translates as 'hall in the wood') to a gate. The house may date from the 16th century and is listed for preservation. Go ahead across lane to go through a gate opposite along a track past farm barns. Continue across stream to join a sunken lane.

In the summer look out for butterflies such as the orange tip, which is cream with distinctive orange wingtips, and the speckled wood, a brown and beige butterfly that thrives on the woodland edge.

At the T-junction, by a timber-framed farm (Sodylt Old Hall) turn right. (NB The footpath does continue along the river but, at time of writing, a bridge over Shell Brook was closed, making the riverside route impassable.)

The central part of Sodylt Old Hall is a cruck-built hall, possibly dating from the 14th century. Along the lane to the right is the larger and later Sodylt Hall. The earliest records found relating to Sodylt appear in a deed between 'Roger Jennings of Sodylt in the township of Dudleston, and Richard & John Chambre of Bolton concerning lands for a pre-nuptual settlement of Roger Jennings and Margret Chambre. In 1795 Sodylt Hall was sold at auctione at the Royal Oak in Ellesmere. There are at least four properties named Sodylt on this lane and, unfortunately it is not clear which property the old records refer to!

4. At the next junction fork left and, at the main B5069 road, turn left again and continue for 700m to Barton's Bridge across Shell Brook. Continue for 100m then take the footpath/track on the left by Barton Cottage. Continue along the cart track with a conifer wood on the right past a white cottage and Knolton Mill (now derelict). The track narrows but runs parallel to Shell Brook. Near the river, ignore the path joining from the bridge on the left, and continue towards the river. Eventually bear right and follow the riverbank, crossing a small bridge to arrive opposite the Boat Inn and Erbistock Church.

The village of Erbistock was reputedly founded by Erbin, a Celtic saint, and the name of the village is thought to be a corruption of "Erbin's Stoke" meaning Erbin's stockaded ford. The Boat Inn is an attractive hostelry built in local red sandstone and has colourful floral displays during the summer. The inn is passed on the next section of the walk and offers a good choice of refreshments. It was originally two buildings that may have been workers cottages and may date from the 16th century, but it was remodelled in the 19th century. It did not become an inn until later in life, and the earliest evidence of a license being obtained is not until 1857.

St Hilary's is the fourth church to be built on this site. The original church was dedicated to Elian ap Erbin (later St. Erbin), a 6th century saint, who survived the massacre at Chester in 616. Very little is known of St. Erbin and it seems likely that the Norman conquerors changed the dedication from a Celtic saint to a Roman one with the same feast day, hence, St. Hilary's Church.

The first written reference to a church in Erbistock is in a taxation record from 1254. The next mention is in 1692, when the building was in danger of collapse. By the mid-18th century a stone church had been built to replace the disintegrating wooden one. About a hundred years later that church was demolished and replaced by the present neo-Gothic building.

The route now continues to follow the river, never veering far from the riverbank. After the Boat Inn keep left to cross a stile into Llan–y-cefn (translates as church ridge) wood.

Beside the River Dee

Erbistock Mill

The wood is rich in wildlife. In spring walkers will see snowdrops, pungent wild garlic, wood anemone, bluebells, marsh marigold, violets, dog's mercury and yellow archangel. In summer the dense overhead foliage keeps the lower vegetation from becoming too overgrown. A variety of insects and fungi thrive in the dead wood and leaves on the woodland floor. Those interested in fungi may notice jew's ear, scarlet elf cup, candle-wick fungus and a variety of polypores.

Continue to cross the next stile and footbridge. At a marker post by a tiny bridge go left over several small footbridges to reach a large open field. This is a flood plain and a former loop of the river. Ignore the path to the right in 400m, which leads to Overton village, and continue along the riverbank, crossing a stile.

Go left along the field boundary to cross next stile. Follow the river to cross a stile to the left of a gate into woodland. Leave the woodland via a double gate and continue ahead, bearing slightly right to an open gate. Follow the footpath left, ignoring the bridleway right.

Note the flood-line marker on the right, opposite Groves Farm, showing how high the waters rose on 9th Feb, 1946!

Go through an old iron gate into woodland past a disused quarry to a gate. Continue ahead past a stile on left from which there are excellent views of Erbistock Mill and weir. Continue past the back of a group of houses to cross a stile by a gate. Go ahead to the road then turn left and along the A539 to Overton Bridge.

Cross Foxes, Overton Bridge

Overton Bridge - Ruabon

Distance: 8.5km (5.3 miles)
Time: 2.5 - 3hrs

A delightful walk along the riverside through Erbistock, then across fields and past the estates of Pen-y-lan and Wynnstay, ending in the historic town of Ruabon.

Parking: Limited parking by Cross Foxes, Overton Bridge, or in the pub car park with the landlord's permission.
Grid ref: SJ354428; **Map:** OS Explorer 256.
Facilities: Pubs in Overton Bridge, Erbistock and Ruabon.
Public transport: None available at time of writing.

The Walk

The current twin arched Overton Bridge was built in 1814 replacing an early single arch bridge, built by a Mr. Penson, that had collapsed. This was not the only one of Mr Penson's creations that lacked stability. He designed the tall obelisk that originally crowned the Jubilee Tower on Moel Famau, but that was struck by lightning and also collapsed!

Beside Overton Bridge is the Cross Foxes Inn. It was built in 1748 by Sir Watkin Williams Wynn for his estate workers, but was later used as a staging post for the Chester-Shrewsbury coach. The crossed foxes are from the Wynn coat of arms.

1. From Overton Bridge follow the road towards Wrexham/ Marchwiel then turn left onto the lane around the back of the

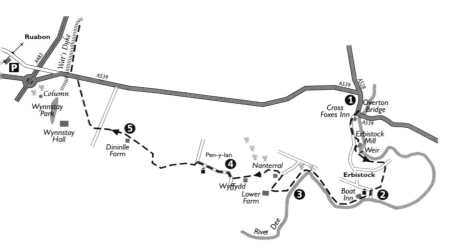

Cross Foxes. Continue along the lane. After about 600m Erbistock Mill and weir may be glimpsed down to the left. Just beyond this point, where a lane joins from the right, turn left to cross a stile by a fingerpost. Go down steps and follow the path down towards the river then U-turn right to follow the riverbank path. Take care along the path, which is slippery after rain.

Wildflowers and ferns thrive in the damp woodland. Most noticeable in spring is the pungent, white-flowered wild garlic and, in late summer, the tall, pink flowered Himalayan balsam dominates. Himalayan balsam is an introduced plant that is now classified as an invasive weed as it can swamp other plants.

Follow the meandering woodland path above the river, crossing footbridges and stiles, finally crossing into a field. Walk directly across the field and go over a stile onto a lane. Cross the lane and then go through the gate/stile opposite. Turn right and follow the right-hand field edge towards a distant wall ahead. Go through the gate/stile at the right end of the field in front of the wall. Turn right to walk up the drive.

St Hilary's Church, Erbistock

2. At the road turn left and follow it into the tiny settlement of Erbistock, which dates from at least 1254, passing St Hilary's Church on the right.

There have been several churches on the site but the present building was started in 1860 as a memorial to Henry Ellis Boates by his wife Caroline. It is a small, neat, sandstone neo-Gothic church with a modest bellcote, which makes its grandiose interior decidedly unexpected. The apse, behind the altar, is continental in appearance with heavy sandstone arches resting on sturdy marble pillars. The tops of the marble pillars are beautifully decorated with a profusion of carved flowers. Look also for the 18th century sundial outside the south porch that is mounted on the shaft of an ancient cross.

Between the church and the Boat Inn turn left down the steps.

These steps led to the ferry across the Dee connecting Erbistock with Overton and Llan-y-cefn. The ferry, which ceased operation in

1939, was a small flat-bottomed boat pulled by cables spanning the river. The old ferry windlass is still visible above the steps. In 1896 over ten thousand passengers are recorded as having crossed the river here.

The Boat Inn was probably built in the 16th century as workers' cottages and didn't become an inn until the 19th century. It is not certain if it is named after the ferry or the Boates family. Another theory is that the original framework of the building was made from old boats as all available new wood was being used to build a fleet to challenge the Spanish Armada.

At the bottom of the steps turn right then cross a stile. Follow the riverside path, crossing another stile, and later, a stile into a wood. Continue along the path, with the river on the left, crossing a bridge by the weir and passing various sandstone outcrops and crossing a number of small bridges. Soon after a scrub island follow a fenceline on the right to another footbridge, by the disused Sodylt Ford.

The River Dee

3. 100m beyond the footbridge turn right over a stile up the slope to cross a further stile, then bear half-left across the field. Go through the gate and follow the left-hand field boundary to a metal gate in front of Lower Farm. Do not go through this gate, instead turn right and follow the fenceline for 100m before veering half-right towards a sunken path, which leads to a stile by a metal gate. Cross the stile and then a stream and, where the path meets the tarmac road, bear left to continue around the house. Go over the stile into the woods. Follow the woodland path, climbing upwards to a sunken track. Follow the way markers along the sunken track. Cross an open field to a double gate (way marker on fence post). Continue to the next stile, keeping the fence on the right. Cross this and continue with the fence on the right, eventually coming to a tarmac lane.

4. Turn right and follow the lane towards Pen-y-lan, passing All Saints Church on the left.

The hamlet of Pen-y-lan was originally an estate village built by the owners of the nearby grand mansion of the same name. The main house may date from the 17th century but was remodelled in grand Georgian style in 1830. A later owner, James Ormrod, generously provided the church of All Saints for public worship in 1889. The dark red sandstone for the building was quarried from his estate and the wood furnishings were made from oak felled on the estate. Inside the church is fine 19th century stained glass illustrating many of the Saints, and antique tiles from the local firm of J. C. Edwards. James Ormond was evidently a philanthropic landlord as he also funded the building of a village school.

Turn left by Quoin Cottage to follow a drive then right after 100m over a stile. Follow the right-hand field boundary up the field through an open gate ahead, then bear slightly left away from the farm track to cross another track then on around the left-side of a pond to cross a stile. Follow right-hand field boundary to gap in far right corner then continue for 50m to cross stile on left. Follow right-hand field boundary to cross a further stile in 20m. Continue along the right-hand field boundary to cross stile on right then follow left-hand boundary to cross stile just to the right of Dininlle Farm and go across the back of the farm.

5. Go left at the access road then almost immediately right over stile. Continue ahead through an open gate then half-left across the next field to join a tarmac lane. Turn left then immediately right by School Lodge and continue to footpath sign on right. Turn right into woodland then follow the indistinct path half-left to cross a stile at the woodland edge. Go ahead, keeping to the left of a pond, to cross a further stile.

The property to the left is Wynnstay Hall, the French Renaissance chateau-style mansion of the Williams Wynn family. The family dominated life around Wrexham in late 18th & 19th centuries as MPs, landowners and patrons. The family's estates covered much of north-east Wales, as hinted in the number of hotels and pubs named the Wynnstay Arms.

A fire in 1858 destroyed Wynnstay Hall. Despite having the wealth needed to build the Victorian replacement, this tragedy heralded the family's loss of power. The present house took over seven years to build. Meanwhile, the Reform Acts weakened the family's political hold on the county of Denbighshire as Parliament began to represent people and not just property. The house was sold in 1947 and became a school, but has since been converted into apartments.

Continue across the field towards the gate house then turn left then right to exit along the drive under the gatehouses arch. Turn left along the main A539, towards Ruabon. Either follow the road into the town or, to continue on the next section of Wat's Dyke Way, take the next kissing gate on the right.

Ruabon - Wrexham

Distance: 7.8 km (4.8 miles)
Time: 2.5 - 3hrs

A mainly level walk beside Wat's Dyke, then through the impressive estate of Erddig Park, finishing at St Giles' Church, Wrexham.

Parking: At the time of writing free parking is available on Station Road but there is also parking in Ruabon centre.
Grid ref: SJ300438 **Map:** OS Explorer 256 1:25 000.
Facilities: Shops & pubs in Ruabon, all facilities in Wrexham.
Public transport: Frequent bus services between Wrexham and Ruabon, X94, X5, 555, 2/2A/2C/2E, also train service.

The Walk

1. From Ruabon station, walk back along Station Road and turn left onto Bridge Street. Continue past the 'Roundhouse', an early 18th century jail with a domed roof used to imprison drunks and undesirables overnight. Just before the Wynnstay Arms, an old coach-house, turn right into Park Street and go past the stone workers' cottages built by the Wynnstay Estate.

On the right is the entrance to Wynnstay Park. The gates, costing £150, were paid for by the people of Ruabon and Wrexham to mark the 21st birthday of the Wynnstay heir in 1912. As you leave Ruabon, in the distance on the right, is the Wynnstay column, commissioned by the mother of the fourth baronet and erected in 1790. The column is 116 feet high, topped with a large bronze vase adorned with goats' heads. The inscription reads, "filio optimo mater

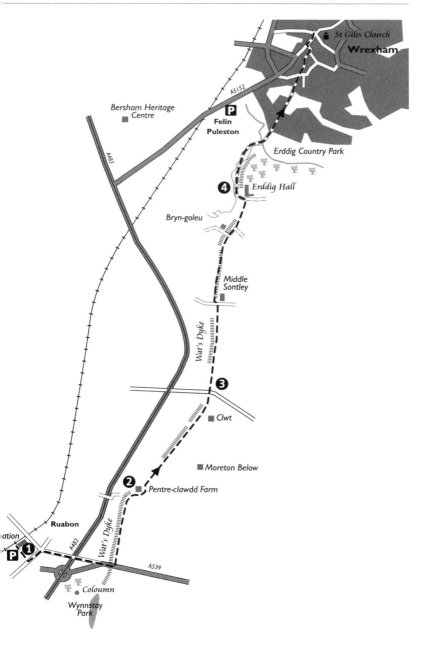

Wynnstay Estate gates

- eheu - supertes" - dedicated to the best of sons by his mother who - alas - survives him.

Cross over the dual carriageway, ignoring the footpath on the left immediately after the bridge, and continue ahead past Vicarage Fields to the crest of the hill.

Turn left through a kissing gate into a field and follow the path alongside a section of Wat's Dyke on the left.

This stretch of Wat's Dyke is particularly well-preserved with the ditch clearly visible to the left of the embankment. The dyke was originally 2 metres high with a 2.5 metre V-shaped ditch on the west side. It was designed to give a commanding view westwards and made use of the natural terrain. At Fron Goch, at the end of this field, it was constructed on the edge of a river terrace with the ditch dug out of a silt flat, whilst at Pentre-clawdd (translates as dyke village), further on, the ditch was dug into a natural hollow.

Lift Bridge, Montgomery Canal

Montgomery Canal

The Boat Inn, Erbistock

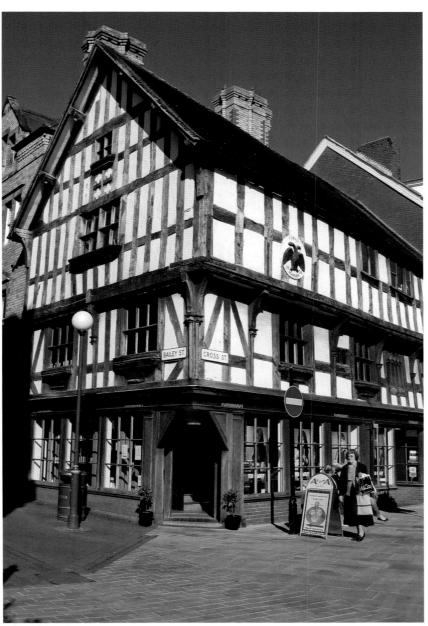

Llwyds' Mansion, Oswestry

Bluebells and stitchwort carpet many of the woodlands in spring

Four spotted chaser dragonfly may be seen around the canal

St Winifred's Well, Woolston

Church of St. Cyngar and St. Cynfach, Hope

turn left after the second stile but continue ahead, passing a large pond on the right, to reach Middle Sontley. Cross the stile in front of the building and turn left for 30m along the lane before turning right over a stile. Follow the right-hand field boundary to cross a double stile. Continue ahead through a large gap in the next hedge to reach a marker post. Go right here over the stile then left to cross a stile opposite Bryn Goleu House. Turn right and follow the tarmac lane into Erddig Park.

The original house at Erddig was designed by Thomas Webb for Joshua Edisbury, High Sheriff of Denbigh, and completed in 1687. The building and furnishing of the house and the laying out of the formal gardens overstretched Edisbury and he was declared bankrupt in 1709. It was sold in 1718 to John Mellor, Master of the Chancery. On his death in 1733 the estate past to his nephew, Simon Yorke, and it remained in Yorke hands until Philip III, the last of the Yorkes, donated it to the National Trust in 1973. The house today gives glimpses of what life was like both above and below stairs. Erddig's walled garden is one of Britain's most important surviving 18th century gardens.

4. Turn left at the signpost to the 'Cup and Saucer' just before the entrance to the house and gardens. Continue to follow the path past gates then bear right, to pass a bridge on the left.

It is worth taking the minor diversion left over the bridge to visit the 'Cup and Saucer', a cascade, that was constructed under the guidance of William Emes, a landscape architect, in 1775. Black Brook gathers in the circular basin, falling over the central weir and exiting through a tunnel a few metres away. It was designed to help prevent erosion by lowering the brook quickly. Next to the Cup and Saucer is a hydraulic ram, installed in 1899, which used the power of the brook to work a pump drawing spring water up 90ft to storage cisterns in the roof of the house. Today it powers the fountains in the garden.

Continue on the main path over two bridges and up the hill past the turning on the left to Felin Puleston.

From Felin Puleston an optional one mile detour, along the Clywedog Trail, leads to Bersham Heritage Centre, which gives an excellent insight into the local iron industry in the 18th and 19th centuries.

5. Go straight on through the kissing gate and barrier to join Erddig Road. Continue past Green Park and Longueville on the left then St Joseph's Catholic and Anglican High School on the right. Cross over Fairy Road and continue along Erddig Road past the Fairfield Tavern, heading towards St Giles church. Go past a car park on the left then along Chapel Street, passing Penybryn Chapel, dated 1789, on the right. Turn right down Bridge Street to the traffic lights. Cross the road and go right along St Giles Way then into a small car park on the left and up some steps to enter St. Giles' Church.

The church steeple was described in the 19th century as one of the Seven Wonders of Wales, along with St Winefride's Well and Overton's Yew trees. It is actually a tower rather than a steeple but is exceptionally fine, richly carved and topped with four hexagonal towers. Standing at 135 foot tall, it is a distinctive landmark in the town.

The church probably stood on the boundary of the original town, which is typical for churches dedicated to St Giles, the patron saint of lepers. The first church may date from as early as the 11th century. In 1330 the original tower collapsed. Reputedly locals feared that God had punished them for having Sunday as their market day and market day was changed to Thursday from then on! However misfortune hit again when fire struck in 1463, destroying much of the church. It was rebuilt between 1463-1520 resulting in the magnificent church that remains today. Not everyone appreciated the church's beauty though - Oliver Cromwell used it to stable his army's horses!

Inside the church the nave ceiling is painted with angels playing celestial music in defiance of Satan's red face, and there are some excellent stained glass windows, a brass eagle lectern and a medieval wall painting of the Day of Judgement above the chancel arch.

In the churchyard, to the south west of the tower, is the grave of Elihu Yale, a local man and benefactor of Yale University, USA.

The Parish Church of St Giles, Wrexham

Wrexham - Caergwrle

Distance: 10.5 km (6.5 miles)
Time: 3.5 - 4hrs

A walk through the historic town of Wrexham, then along sections of Wat's Dyke, the banks of the River Alyn and quiet country lanes to Alyn Waters Country Park, ending in Caergwrle with its 13th century Welsh castle.

Parking: Car park below St.Giles' Church, Wrexham.
Grid ref: SJ335501; **Map:** OS Explorer 256.
Facilities: All in Wrexham, pubs and shops in Caergwrle.
Public transport: No 26 bus between Wrexham and Caergwrle, also train service.

The Walk

1. This walk starts in Wrexham from St Giles' Church.

Wrexham developed from a medieval market town, into a thriving industrial centre in the 18th and 19th centuries as a result of iron, coal and lead mining. Nowadays it is a prime shopping centre. Brewing became important from the late 18th century, with 19 breweries in the town by the 1880s! It was later home to the first lager brewery in Britain.

Leave via the main gates and go along Church Street passing College Street on the left.

The Welsh name for College Street was Camfa'r Cwn meaning the

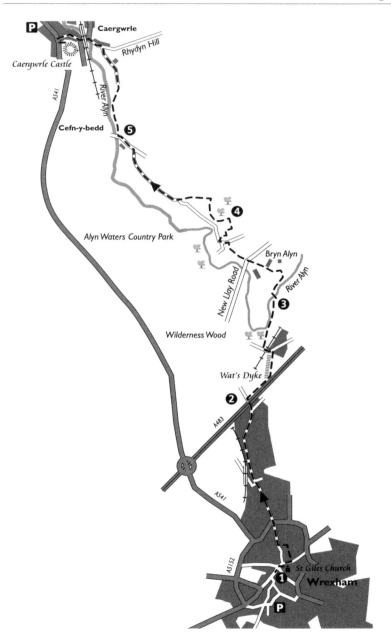

Dog's Stile. Perhaps there was a stile to keep the dogs out of the churchyard at this location?

Turn right along High Street, away from the town centre.

The old Town Hall once stood at the junction of High Street, Church Street and Hope Street but was demolished in 1940. In 1583 Saint Richard Gwynn, a Catholic priest, was held here, in the Black Chamber (Y Siambr Ddu), before being hung, drawn and quartered on the site of Eagles Meadow development. Charles I also reputedly addressed the people of Wrexham from the Town Hall.

Towards the end of the street on the left is the attractive entrance to the Butchers' Market, which was the supermarket of the 19th century. Its grand Neo-Jacobean style made a bold statement to people entering that shopping here would be a quality experience. Inside the original building a large room on the first floor housed the Corn Exchange and it also had its own inn.

Turn left at the end of High Street in front of the Wynnstay Arms to go along Chester Street.

In February 1876 local football enthusiasts founded the Football Association of Wales in the Wynnstay Arms and organised the first national football team to represent Wales. The hotel was formerly known as the Eagles Inn (from which Eagles Meadow takes its name), and, in 1892, had 8 acres of land. Its entrance was "lined with stuffed birds and stags' heads" and there was stabling for 200 horses.

Continue up Chester Street passing Henblas Street on the left.

Henblas was another market area in the 19th century with traders coming from Birmingham, Manchester and Yorkshire to sell their wares. In 1879 a Butter Market was built here and local farmers' wives competed to sell their dairy produce direct to the customer. Rationing in 1939 ended the tradition of farmhouse butter and the Butter Market became the canteen for the US Army Medical Corps

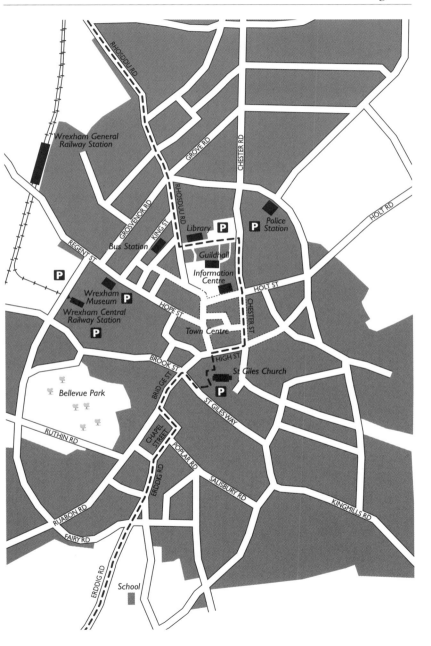

during the Second World War. Henblas Street was a place of entertainment too; the Hippodrome, which was a variety theatre from 1909, showed the first "talkie" in Wrexham in 1929.

Carry on up Chester Street past Lambpit Street and the Seven Stars Pub.

Many think the name Lambpit comes from a lime pit formerly in this area. Next to the pub is the old Glyn Cinema that claimed to be the first purpose-built cinema in North Wales.

Look out for Chester Street Baptist Chapel on the left. Wrexham has been home to a Baptist community since 1672. In the early years they suffered a lot of discrimination both from the state and local people. In 1762 the Baptists finally built a permanent chapel on Chester Street. They called it the 'Old Meeting' to celebrate their origins when they worshipped in private homes. The original chapel was demolished in 1875.

Ahead on the right, beyond the chapel, is the Goscombe John Memorial to the Royal Welch Fusiliers killed in the First World War. The tall building in the distance on the right is the Police Station. If you are lucky you might see the peregrine falcons that nest on top.

Before reaching the war memorial turn left to pass through the old gateway to Llwyn Isaf towards the Guildhall.

Llwyn Isaf is now a green space in the heart of the town and the outside living room for Yale College students. Originally there was a house on this site known as Ysbyty Ucha (Upper Hospital) - a name hinting at a possible monastic past. In the 19th century the house was called Llwyn Isaf and became home to the vicars of Wrexham.

The 1912 National Eisteddfod was proclaimed here, though David Lloyd George got a rough reception from the Suffragettes, who were angry with the Liberal Government's opposition to votes for women.

Continue on the footpath between the Guildhall and the

Library, a modern brick building with a colourful mosaic on the side. Turn right and head up Rhosddu Road passing Trinity Presbyterian Church of Wales on the left. At the roundabout, keep straight ahead.

On the right is the attractive façade of what is now Yale College. In 1918 the people of Wrexham decided to mark the sacrifice of local servicemen who had died during the First World War by building a new hospital. The Prince of Wales laid the foundation stone on November 2nd 1923 and the hospital served the local community for sixty years. It survived planned demolition and is now home to Yale College. Near the college entrance is a wellhead from one of Wrexham's old wells and nearby are some pillar bases that may have come from the old Town Hall.

A local resident, William Low, set up the Channel Tunnel Company in 1867. His plan to build a tunnel under the English Channel got backing from Emperor Napoleon III of France and Queen Victoria. He began tunnelling but the Franco-Prussian war in 1870 frightened off investors and the project folded.

Alyn Waters Country Park

At the next roundabout continue straight on.

On the left is Grosvenor Road that was originally a ropewalk where cordswainers made their ropes.

Eventually Rhosddu Road joins New Road. Continue on this road, crossing over the busy A483 dual carriageway.

2. Immediately after crossing the A483 turn right down steps, at a footpath sign, then cross a stile. Walk parallel to the A483 for 300m. At the end of the left-hand fence, go half-left for 100m to a wooden stile on the right (NB: This area can be extremely waterlogged in wet periods). Cross stile and follow left-hand field boundary over two stiles to reach Plas Acton Road. Cross the road but ignore the waymarked path opposite, instead turn left across the railway bridge then right into Pandy Industrial Estate. Continue ahead to cross a stile by a gate then go ahead, bearing left down an indistinct path immediately after the Pandy Waste Water Pumping Station (ignore main track bearing right). Descend down the slope into Wilderness Wood and turn right at the stream along wooden boardwalks. Continue then cross a stile then half-right before a pond, up the slope. Cross a further stile and turn left along the track then over a bridge and stile.

3. Turn right over cattle grid to follow tarmac access road away from Wilderness Farm. At the junction with Pont-y-Capel Lane turn left uphill to cross a stile on left after 50m. Follow this path up the slope to emerge in a field with a house (Bryn Alyn) ahead to the right. Go across field to stile. Cross stile and bear right to hidden stile to left of house. Cross lane then stile opposite. Go half-left across field to kissing gate then down slope to cross New Llay Road. Continue up the opposite slope via a footpath immediately on the left. Ignore first stile on right and continue along the top of woods with green fence on right to a second stile. Cross this stile then go half-left to a stile on the right of a white house.

4. Cross stile and turn left along a tarmac road. Ignore the lane on the left and turn right into Alyn Waters Country Park.

Alyn Waters Country Park, on the banks of the River Alyn, was once the site of a sand and gravel quarry, but in the last 10 years thousands of trees have been planted to help nature reclaim the area, transforming it into Wrexham's largest country park.

Follow the tarmac cycle track to wooden benches and a white marble sculpture then turn left onto a gravel path. At second bench keep left continuing on the gravel path. After the next bench by a marker post, with DO etched on it, go left through an Active Lifestyles Project Area to re-join the cycle track. Turn left to exit the park through barriers onto Park Road. Turn right and follow the lane for about 1 km, past a pond, then turn left along the B5102, Llay Road.

5. Take the waymarked footpath on the right by a Flintshire County Council boundary sign. Follow this well-defined path above the River Alyn. After 500m cross a stile up the right bank then go half-left across an open field to a wooden bridge. Cross bridge and go half-right to cross a stile on the right of a white house. At footpath junction bear left through the trees to cross another wooden bridge. Follow the path/bridleway to a metalled road (Rhyddyn Hill).

On the left by the River Alyn is the site of the old Caergwrle Spa. First mentioned in 1740, the site was developed in the early 1900s using two local springs whose waters were claimed to have healing and restorative properties. A pump house, bottling house, tea room, and bandstand were built and a bowling green laid out. Trains brought tourists to the village from Liverpool, Manchester and the Midlands.

6. Turn left down the hill then left onto the A541 (Hawarden Road). Turn right on Castle Street to enter Caergwrle with its choice of pubs and shops.

Caergwrle derives it's name from a combination of Welsh and old English terms; caer (fort) + corn (crane, heron) + lea (glade, clearing) thus fort by the heron's glade.

Turn left by the phone box then left again just before the war memorial to follow a path uphill. Climb steps and bear right along path up more steps, then follow clear path to the castle ruins on the hilltop.

The dominant feature above the village is the castle built by Dafydd ap Grufydd in 1278. It was probably used as a base for his attack on the English castle at Hawarden in March 1282. By the time Edward I's troops reached Caergwrle in June 1282 they found that Dafydd had dismantled his own castle, blocked the well, and fled.

After exploring the castle retrace your steps to the war memorial. Turn right and go up the High Street to continue on Wat's Dyke Way.

Caergwrle Castle

Caergwrle - New Brighton

Distance: 13.2 km (8.2 miles)
Time: 3 - 3.5hrs

A fairly flat walk from the historic village of Caergwrle using lanes and across farmland, including a well-preserved section of Wat's Dyke, ending at New Brighton. NB This section is more suburban than most of the others.

Parking: Car park in Caergwrle.
Grid ref: SJ 335501; **Map:** OS Explorer 256 and 266.
Facilities: Pubs and shops in Caergwrle, Hope, Mynydd Isa and New Brighton.
Public transport: No 26 bus between Mold and Caergwrle.

The Walk

1. From the car park cross the High Street and turn left in front of a brick chapel then turn right before the stone chapel onto Fellows Lane. At the T-junction continue ahead down a narrow path beside the Derby Arms to the packhorse bridge.

The area to the right of the Derby Arms was the site of the Caergwrle Brewery founded in 1861. The local spa waters were highly valued for brewing.

The 17th century packhorse bridge was built to allow packhorse trains travelling between Corwen and Chester to cross the river when it was in full spate. The walls were low to allow for the horses' bulging packs and the v-shaped bays gave pedestrians space to wait if they met packhorses whilst crossing the bridge.

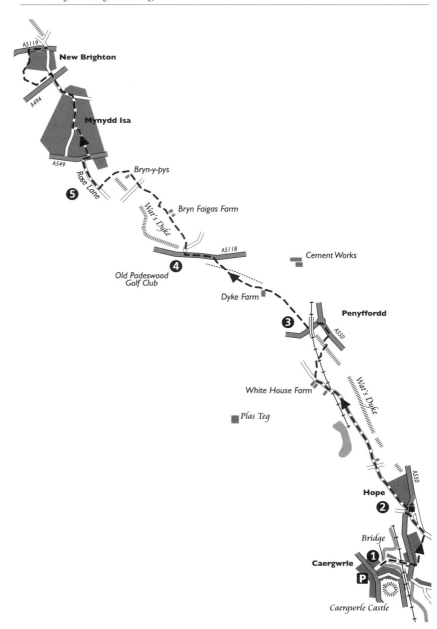

The Packhorse Bridge, Caergwrle

Cross the packhorse bridge and continue up Fellows Lane over the railway bridge to the main A550 road. Cross the road and walk up the drive opposite. At the entrance to Rhyddyn Farm (white house) turn right up steps and over stile then walk left along fence line. At the fence corner follow footpath signed ahead, walking uphill, to a kissing gate.

Go through the kissing gate and turn left. The raised bank on which you are now walking is part of Wat's Dyke. Follow the fenced path via a small gate and two kissing gates through to Gresford Road. Turn left along road and then left down a minor lane immediately after. Continue along this residential lane (Kiln Lane) to Hope Church.

Hope Church, dedicated to St. Cyngar and St. Cynfach, is considered to be the oldest church in Flintshire. The remains of a Celtic cross, discovered during the 2000 restoration, suggest that the site has been a place of worship since the 9th or 10th centuries. The present structure dates from 1180 to 1500. The church had strong ties

Church of St. Cyngar and St. Cynfach, Hope

with the Trevor family from Plas Teg Hall, which can be seen later on the route, and the south aisle of the church became the Trevor Chapel in the early 17th century.

2. From the church steps cross the road and continue ahead along Stryt Isa, passing the school and playing fields on the left. At the cross roads with Pigeon House Lane continue ahead. Continue along Stryt Isa for about 2.3 miles with good views left to the Clwydian Hills. The large house visible in the distance after a mile on the left is Plas Teg.

Plas Teg is one of the most important Jacobean-style houses in Wales, built around 1610 by John Trevor. It utilises the Renaissance concept of symmetry, of proportion and elegance. The house remained in the family until it was sold just after the Second World War to auctioneers who used it as a furniture store! By the mid 1950s it was in a state of advanced decay and its owners applied to demolish it but were refused following a public outcry. It was then bought and partially restored by Patrick Trevor-Roper, a direct descendant of the original owners. It was fully restored to its former glory after it was bought by Cornelia Bayley, a London antiques dealer and interior designer, in 1986. The house is also renowned for being one of the most haunted houses in Wales.

Stryt Isa eventually crosses over the railway, which first came to Hope & Caergwrle in 1866. Continue for a further 300m to reach White House Farm on the left.

Just after White House Farm turn right through a gate by a fingerpost. Follow the left-hand field boundary, passing a wet area on the left. Cross a stile in the far corner of the field. Walk up the railway embankment to carefully cross the line then go over the ladder stile. Follow the left-hand field boundary to go through an open gateway then follow the right-hand boundary to cross a stile. Go half-left towards a telegraph pole then continue across field to cross a stile in the hedge to the right of a gate. Follow the left-hand field boundary to cross a stile then follow the right-hand boundary and cross a stile onto the road. Turn left along A550 to the roundabout then turn left along A5104, signed Corwen. Continue for about 100m then cross the road into Penyffordd Station.

Penyffordd (translates as head of the road) has developed from a small hamlet into a commuter village. In the 19th century the construction of two railways lines led to the establishment of an oil distillation works and a small brickyard.

3. Cross the railway line to the left of the platform then go through a gate and walk in front of Station Cottage. Go through a gate/stile and follow the left-hand boundary across a long field.

The obvious ditch and bank on the left is the remains of Wat's Dyke.

Cross a stile, bear right for a few paces, then follow left-hand field boundary. Cross a stile then a footbridge and a second stile. Turn left and walk along left-hand field boundary, continuing through an open gateway and keeping the Castle Cement tower on the right.

The large tower was part of a controversial £48million development at Castle Cement. By burning used tyres amongst other waste products, the new kiln has provided one solution for the disposal of whole tyres, which were banned from landfill sites in 2003.

Continue through another gate and stile then bear half-right, passing farm buildings with wooden fencing on the left and follow the fence to cross a stile/gate. Continue following the left-hand field boundary down a long field and go through another stile/gate. Partway down the next field turn left over a stile immediately past a cottage then turn right walking with hedge on the right. Cross a small stream and another stile in field corner. Continue walking along the right-hand field boundary. Cross a stile and climb the bank to cross the disused railway. Go through an old kissing gate on the opposite side then turn left and walk alongside the old railway. Just beyond a telegraph pole turn half-right across the field to cross a stile by a fingerpost onto the road. Cross the road and turn left along the verge past Station Road and Padeswood Golf course on right.

4. Take the first right up Padeswood Road South, signed Buckley 1 mile. Turn left before houses over a stile and head up the field to cross a further stile by gate. Follow left-hand field boundary through two more fields, crossing two more stiles then continue ahead through an open gateway. Bear half-left across the field and through a second open gateway then right over a stile a few paces later. Walk uphill past a green log store to cross drive and stile opposite. Walk half-left across the field heading to far left-hand corner and cross stile 100m from corner. Go ahead to opposite field boundary then turn left through an open gateway, passing a farm on right, eventually

Looking towards Moel Famau

crossing a stile by gate onto the road. Cross road and continue over stile opposite beside drive to Bryn y Pys. Follow the right-hand hedge, passing the farm buildings and fenced compound on the left. Continue ahead over a stile and walk along an enclosed path. Turn left at the end, ignoring stile on right, and follow path behind houses. Cross another stile and follow path between a paddock and housing. Continue along right-hand field edge then go over a metal stile. Follow the left-hand field edge through next field, cross a footbridge, continue across the next field and over a stile onto Rose Lane.

5. Turn right and continue along Rose Lane to road junction. Cross the road and turn right. After 100m turn left along Mercia Drive following signs to village centre. Continue past the Mercia Inn & shops/library on left to turn right along Chamber Lane at the T-junction then uphill into Bryn y Baal past Mynydd Isa Junior School. Immediately after crossing over the busy A494 turn left by a footpath fingerpost and walk along a rough gravel track. At next gate turn right over stile and continue to cross a further gate and stile. Do not follow the footpath arrows instead follow the right-hand field boundary to the edge of a barn at Argoed Farm. Turn right over a stile then follow the left-hand field boundary to the cross the next stile. Continue up the right-hand field boundary, past the playing field on the right, to turn right over a stile into a passage between panel fences at the rear of houses. Before barriers turn left and continue along Argoed Avenue to meet the A5119 Main Road. Turn right and continue to the Beaufort Palace Hotel in New Brighton.

The Welsh name for New Brighton is Pentre Cythraul which translates as devil village!

New Brighton - Rhosesmor

Distance: 9.5km (5.9 miles)
Time: 2.5 - 3hrs

A pleasant walk along lanes, through woodland and across fields finishing at Moel y Gaer Iron Age hillfort

Parking: Beaufort Park Hotel (with permission).
Grid ref: SJ 254655; Map: O S Explorer 265 & 266.
Facilities: Hotel, pub and shop in New Brighton, shop & pub in Rhosesmor.
Public Transport: No 126 Rhosesmor - Mold bus service.

The Walk

1. From the traffic lights in New Brighton head away from the Rose & Crown pub along New Brighton Road, passing the Beaufort Park Hotel on the right. Ignore the first turning right immediately after the hotel. Continue along the road turning right at a footpath sign just beyond 'The Cottage'. (Path can be muddy). Cross plank bridge and turn left to cross a metal stile. Keep to the right of the pond, heading to the far right-hand field corner. Cross the stile into a playing field. Follow the right-hand field boundary past a small car park on the left. Join the road ahead, called Wat's Dyke Way, through Sychdyn to the junction with Vownog Newydd. Cross the road and follow a gravel track. Go through a kissing gate on the right of some bungalows and then through a second kissing gate. Turn left and follow the left hand field boundary to the road, going through another kissing gate by a gate.

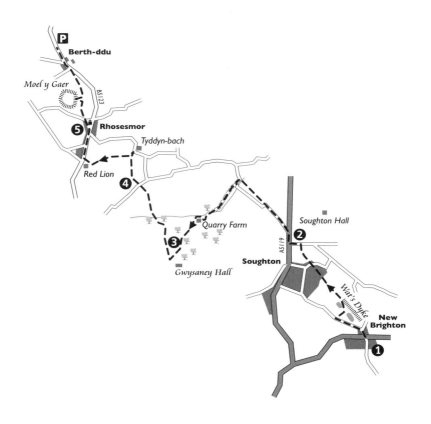

Ahead and to the right is Soughton Hall that has been owned by the Bankes family from the mid 1700's. Today it is a hotel with an attractive restaurant and bar in the converted stable block. Sychdyn is perhaps better known as the home of footballer, Michael Owen!

2. Turn left past the entrance to Coed Andrew and continue to the A5119. Turn right and walk along pavement towards Flint/Northop. Cross road with care to take the first left and continue along the small lane past Clawdd-Offa Farm.

The name Clawdd Offa Farm suggests some connection with Offa's

A well-preserved section of Wat's Dyke, near Sychdyn

Dyke. Its course through northern Flintshire is not clear and some have suggestioned that it may have joined Wat's Dyke for the final 13 miles to the coast.

Where the road bears sharply left cross the stile to the right of the white house and continue along grassy path. Cross two further stiles into fields, passing a pond on the right. Continue ahead along a ridge (this is the bank of Wat's Dyke), with a large stone house below on the left, to a third stile. Cross this and continue ahead, ignoring the stile on the left, following the left-hand fenceline, to a stile and small bridge. Cross these and then turn left onto a lane. In about 150m take the first track on the right by finger post. Continue on this track through a wooded area for just under 1km to Quarry Farm. Pass to the right of the farm through two gate/stiles. After the second turn left and follow the fence line up the field to cross a stile into Ram Wood. Continue through wood to a kissing gate.

Beyond the kissing gate on the left is Gwysaney Hall estate. Gwysaney Hall is a fine Welsh country house, built by Robert Davies in the early 17th century. It has had a chequered history; it was attacked by Roundheads during the Civil War, then abandoned for 200 years before being restored.

3. Continue along the track towards a gate. Just before the gate turn round and walk diagonally left across the large field, passing to the left of a small derelict barn. Head to the left of a large pine that comes into view to find a stile in the opposite field boundary.

There are good views of the Clwydian Range and, in summer harebells and ox-eye daisies edge the field.

Cross the stile, with an open gateway by a large tree to the left, then go half-left across the corner of this field to cross a stile by a gate. Cross the next field to the opposite boundary to find a stile slightly to the right hidden by undergrowth. Cross this into Coed Bryn-eithin (translates as Gorse Hill Wood) and descend through the trees (path is not obvious here). Cross a private track and follow path opposite to leave the wood via a stile and small plank bridge. Bear half-left uphill through field then cross a stile at the top of the slope. Walk across the field to a stile in the far left-hand corner. Cross the stile and then follow the left-hand field boundary to cross a stile onto Eurgain Lane.

4. Cross the lane and stile opposite and follow the right-hand field boundary through a gate / stile, then continue over three more stiles, along the right-hand field boundaries, heading for the farm buildings ahead. Go through the gate in front of the farm and turn left to join a track. Continue on track then go through the middle gate of a group to continue in the same direction up the field, following the left-hand boundary. At the top of the field turn left through a gate and then over the stile opposite. Turn right and follow the right-hand field boundary to cross a stile/gate to join a track next to a house. Follow this track past a garage/workshop to the Red Lion pub. Turn right along the B5123, once the main Shrewsbury to Holyhead road, and follow this towards the village centre.

Rhosesmor expanded greatly during the 19th century lead-mining boom. Mines and lead-processing works once dominated the site of the current industrial estate (Tiger Tim's). The open common is dotted with conical stone structures that cap the numerous mine shafts. There are also the remains of several early quarries and limekilns where crushed limestone was burned to produce lime for building mortar and fertiliser. There is a well-preserved single limekiln on the west side of Moel y Gaer at Wern-y-Gaer.

5. At the crossroads by the phone box turn left across the B5123 and take the side road to the left of the church. Just beyond the church at the next road junction continue ahead on a gravel track, passing to the right of Rock Cottage. Follow the well-defined path contouring the lower slopes of Moel y Gaer Iron Age hillfort.

Single limekiln, Wern-y-Gaer

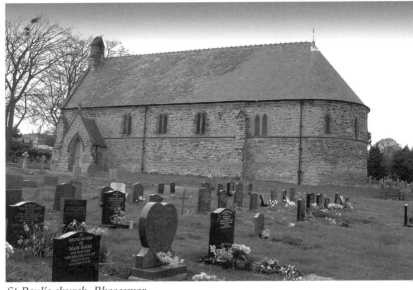

St Paul's church, Rhosesmor

St. Paul's church was consecrated on 21 April 1876, built to accommodate the rapidly growing population when lead-mining was at its peak.

(It is well worth a short detour to the top of Moel y Gaer to enjoy the views. To do this turn left and follow the path up the hillside, passing a small quarry on the left. This leads to what was the main entrance to the hillfort. Retrace your steps to rejoin the main route. For further information on the hillfort please refer to Walk 3, Rhosesmor Circular.)

When the grassy path joins a gravel track dog-leg right and head towards the bus stop and Rhos Helyg School Continue ahead to reach the B5123 again by the school. At the main road turn left and continue past the school to the viewpoint layby at Berth Ddu. To continue with the next section of the route turn right after the bungalow, Garreg Lwyd.

Rhosesmor - Holywell

Distance: 14.5km (9 miles)
Time: 4.5 - 5 hrs

A gentle walk from the open common of Halkyn Mountain across fields, woodland and along lanes down to Holywell, visiting St Winefride's Well, and exploring Holywell's industrial past in Greenfield Heritage Park, before ending at the ruins of Basingwerk Abbey.

Parking: Viewpoint layby on B5123, Rhosesmor to Halkyn road, north of Rhos Helyg School.
Grid Ref: SJ 209698; **Map:** OS Explorer 265.
Facilities: Pub in Rhosesmor and Halkyn, all facilities in Holywell, and toilets, information centre and café at Greenfield Heritage Park.
Public Transport: No 126 Holywell - Rhosesmor bus service.

The Walk

1. From the layby turn left (when facing the road) and walk along road towards Rhosesmor. Turn left before bungalow 'Garreg Lwyd' (before Rhos Helyg School) and cross an area known as Pen-y-parc.

Pen-y-parc is an 18th century farm whose land included a deer park, developed by Lord Grosvenor in 1761. Sections of the eight foot high stone wall that once enclosed the deer park still remain.

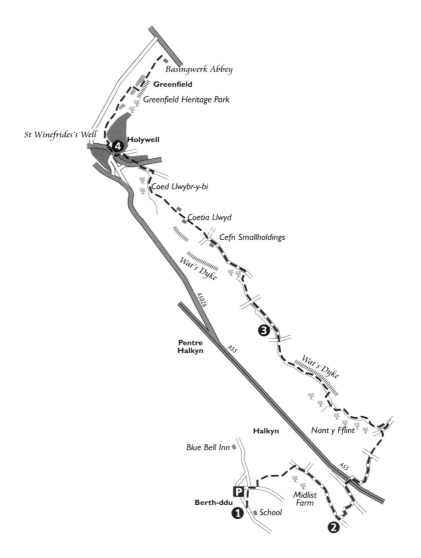

When the wall on right ends continue ahead. Cross a gravel lane and continue ahead on gravel track. At a converted chapel turn right down tarmac lane, then at footpath sign turn left away from lake to cross metal stile in far right corner. Follow left-hand boundary over two stiles enjoying wide views across the Dee Estuary. Follow the line of the telegraph poles down the field to cross a wooden stile hidden in the corner. Go ahead with a small copse on the left to a reach a concrete track to Midlist Farm, and then turn left towards the pond. Cross cattle grid at end of farm track and turn right onto tarmac lane. When lane turns sharp left continue ahead on gravel then grass track, with woodland and the river, Afon Conwy, on the right.

The track and lane are part of the old coach road, which ran from Chester via Halkyn to Holywell, until it was replaced by the original A55 that was built in 1826-7.

2. At bridleway sign turn left to continue along a sunken lane between two hedges to the main road. Cross road and turn left. Turn right over the bridge to cross over the busy A55 dual-carriageway. Follow the lane around to the right and then left, ignoring the entrance to Coed-y-cra Uchaf (a fine 17th century house) and the path opposite. At crossroads continue ahead on gravel bridleway past a black bollard onto a leafy sunken lane to reach a tarmac road. Turn right downhill then left over stile by footpath fingerpost. Go to left of black corrugated barn over stile and footbridge then uphill to enter woodland, Coed y Cra. After 500m when path forks go left and descend downhill to cross a large footbridge. Continue up the opposite bank of the stream to emerge by a black and white building, Nant Mill. Turn right and follow gravel track above Nant-y-Flint which soon becomes a green lane. Cross second footbridge back over the stream to cross two stiles. Continue now on this delightful path through the narrow wooded valley above Nant-y-Flint passing through an area of rhododendron and holly. At a marker post continue left. Continue to cross metal stile then at next marker post continue ahead (ignoring gate on right) to cross a wooden stile onto a concrete path by the stream, which leads to a further stile onto a tarmac road.

View across the Dee Estuary

3. Turn right then almost immediately left along Nant Road. Continue for 750m past the ponds by Nant Farm and Bethel Chapel, built in 1847, to the junction of Nant Road and Bryn Tirion. Continue ahead for about 500m then cross stile on right before final house (Nant Bach) and go up slope to another stile. Continue ahead uphill then over stile in hedge opposite. Turn left along tarmac lane. Ignore Gadlys Lane joining from right.

Gadlys was once the site of a prestigious lead smelting and silver refining works in the 18th century. Lead from here was sent by ship to Plymouth and London. Also close by is Bryn Dychwelwch (Hill of Return), the site of a famous battle in 1157, which resulted in Henry II having to retreat from the Welsh forces.

Continue along Cefn Lane past Cefn Farm on right and past a green corrugated barn at Cefn Smallholdings to reach a sharp left-hand bend. Cross the stile opposite by the millennium cycleway sign. Initially follow the left-hand field boundary then go half-right to cross a stile by a tree. Go ahead across the next field to cross a stile then follow right-hand field boundary

St Winefride's Well

towards buildings. In the far right-hand corner cross the stile on right then almost immediately the stile on left. Then cross the bottom of the garden of Coetia Llwyd and go over a further stile. Follow the right-hand field boundary, crossing a stile by some derelict buildings.

There are good views to the mouth of the Dee Estuary and Irish Sea on right. On clear days Blackpool Tower and even the Lake District Fells are visible.

Continue along right hand boundary over a stile to reach a stile on the edge of Coed Llwybr-y-bi. Cross stile and descend slope turning right just before the stream to join a path, which contours the slope. At an obvious junction turn left down some steps again towards the stream. At the bottom go half-right to leave the wood via a kissing gate onto a tarmac lane. Turn left over bridge then up the hill. Just before the lane reaches the main A5026 road go left up some steps and cross the road here. Continue up the road opposite (Rose Hill) then left along Pen-y-Maes Road to arrive at a small car park on the right.

4. Go through the car park and cross Strand Walk, heading towards the prominent Tesco store. Take first right down the slope into Tesco's car park, bearing half-left to a Croeso/Welcome sign. Here descend a slope and continue to go under a double-arched bridge along a disused railway line.

Built in 1869 the railway track was originally used to transport minerals from local quarries to Greenfield Wharf. In 1913 it changed to passenger use and has carried many thousands of pilgrims to St Winefride's Well until it closed to passengers in 1954. With a 1:27 gradient it was the steepest conventional railway in Britain.

Continue for 500m along the disused railway line until you pass a block of sandstone on the left. At the next junction turn left, almost back on yourself, to go through a black metal kissing gate then bear right towards the main B5121 road. At the road turn left to visit St Winifred's Well, which is 100m further on.

St Winefride's Well, the holy well, which gave the town its name, is sited within a 15th century chapel. The legend of the well began in 660AD when Prince Caradoc tried to seduce the beautiful Gwenffrewi or Winefride. When she refused and escaped, Caradoc pursued her and cut off her head. Her uncle, St Beuno, reunited her head with her body. Water gushed from the ground where her head had fallen. The shrine became one of the great places of pilgrimage in the Christian world and immersion in the well is believed to have powers of healing.

Retrace your steps, turning right out of St.Winefride's Well, then right again in 100m, back to the kissing gate. Take the left-hand path entering Greenfield Heritage Park, passing a tall chimney on the left. At the next junction turn left and descend the steps to the Royal Oak car park then turn right at 'Mount Cilead' sign, keeping the Battery Pool then Greenfield Mill on the right.

The Battery Works have a poignant history. Established in 1776, they employed local people to shape pots and pans. The products were made by 'battering' sheets of copper and brass with large hammers. The goods were exported through Liverpool to Africa, and used as payment for slaves, who were taken to America to work in the cotton fields. The cotton was then brought back for processing, ensuring that the ships always had a full cargo.

Go past the dam wall on the right. At next junction keep left passing a disused clock tower on the left. Go through a kissing gate into a small car park. Bear half-right through the car park then down wooden steps. Turn right to cross the dam wall of Meadow Mill Pond. At the end of the dam cross the metal gratings over the weir, then go down the metal steps before turning left down wooden steps to the bottom of the weir. Follow the path through the remains of Old Meadow Mill.

Lower Cotton Mill

Meadow Mill was built in 1787 to manufacture copper rollers for printing patterns onto cloth. Three enormous waterwheels, 20 feet in diameter, provided the power for the copper rolling machinery. The buildings that remain today date from the 1800s when there was a rubber grinding and tin plate works on site.

Continue past a sculpture entitled 'Old Story, New Story' by Lorna Green, which incorporates two large gates that were once part of the Grosvenor Charter Paper Works. The title reflects old coming around to the new and refers to the valley change of usage from an industrial site to a place for nature and pleasure now. It also refers to the gates once being used as an entrance to a factory, now being re-used within a sculpture.

Continue along, passing a further mill pond on the left then join the tarmac road. Continue past the Lower Cotton Mill on the left.

The large rectangular ruin is the remains of the six-storey cotton mill *built here in just 10 weeks in 1785 by John Smalley. The Cotton Twist Company employed up to 300 apprentices, many of them under 10 years old. The cotton mill closed in 1840 but it reopened as a Victoria Corn Mill in 1850, producing flour until the early 1900's. The old mill warehouse was restored in 1982. Today it houses a steam pop bottling plant - another industry that flourished in the Valley.*

A little further, on the left, is the impressive pit for the waterwheel that powered the machinery for Abbey Mill, which produced copper and brass wire for making nails and pins.

Turn right just before the Environment Centre and continue past some old lead-mining wagons to the old school. Turn right towards the Visitor Centre and then on to reach the end of Wat's Dyke Way at Basingwerk Abbey.

Basingwerk Abbey dates from 1132. The monks were Cistercian, known as White Monks, from the colour of their habits. They used the power of the stream to grind corn and also mined lead and silver, making the Abbey rich and powerful. Henry VIII's Dissolution Act finally drove the monks out of the Abbey in 1536.

The ruins of Basingwerk Abbey

Queen's Head Circular

Distance: 11.0 km (6.8 miles)
Time: 3.0 – 3.5 hrs

From Queen's Head this walk crosses Oswestry Golf course then continues through fields and along quiet lanes into Maesbury Marsh, then briefly follows the course of Wat's Dyke before returning along the Montgomery Canal towpath, with a diversion to visit St Winifred's Well at Woolston.

Parking: Small car park opposite the Queen's Head pub.
Grid ref: SJ339268 **Map:** OS Explorer 240 Oswestry.
Facilities: Pubs in Queen's Head and Maesbury Marsh, cafe/shop (Canal Central), near Maesbury Marsh.

The Walk

1. From the car park turn left along B5009 then left again for a short distance then cross the busy A5, with care. Trn right then left up the driveway to Oswestry Golf Club. Head to the rear of the club car park then go across the front of the Club House. Turn left initially following the line of a conifer hedge. Follow a small valley downhill, keeping to the right-hand side of the thicket out of the fairway. Continue in this direction following the footpath marker posts. Bear half-right at the back of the tee for hole 17 to a sunken path on the horizon. Continue ahead to cross a footbridge. Go ahead over a further stile into a small wood. Walk through the wood, passing a small pond on the

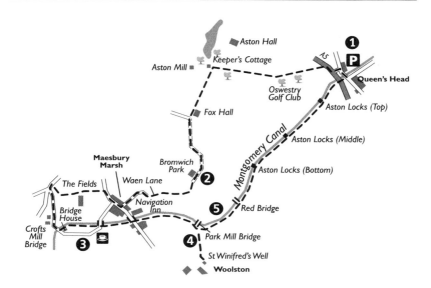

right. At the woodland edge go a further 40m to cross a stile into a field, with views of Aston Hall to the right.

18th century Aston Hall is a Grade II listed country house. During its time, it has been a hospital and a school, but has now reverted to domestic use. The house is set in a fine park with a large lake immediately to the west. It was home to Lieutenant General Sir Francis Lloyd who was tasked by Lord Kitchener to raise 'a Welsh regiment of foot guards'. He accepted the challenge promising that 'The Welsh Guards' would mount 'King's Guard' at Buckingham Palace two days later, on St. David's Day. They did this, though still wearing the uniforms of their old regiments.

Head for the far left-hand corner then turn left over a stile. Follow left-hand field boundary to cross a small field behind Keeper's Cottage. Go through the gates in opposite boundary. Follow track along left-hand field boundary over stile.

To the right is the site of 19th century Aston Watermill, used to grind corn from the local farms.

Continue along the left-hand field boundary past Fox Hall to cross a stile in the hedge on the left. Turn right down the drive away from the hall. Follow this lane past Bromwich Park.

Bromwich Park has a good example of a medieval moat, of particular interest because of its association with the remains of a later formal garden.

2. About 200m after Bromwich Park, follow the track right towards Maesbury Marsh along Waen Lane. When joining the main Maesbury Road turn right then second left to follow a track to go past 'The Fields'.

'The Fields' is a farm thought to date from Anglo-Saxon times when they grew crops and kept livestock in 'the fields' outside the fortified settlement a little to the north. The current house probably dates from the 18th century, but there would have been previous dwellings on the same site for many centuries.

The Montgomery Canal, near Maesbury Marsh

At the farm buildings, the track goes to the left. Turn right through a gateway, then immediately left at way marker, along a narrow path around fields, then cross stream and on through wet meadow. Turn right to cross over stile into a field then left along field edge to exit onto road. Turn left over bridge and then first left down Coed y Rae Lane. (Coed y Rae Lane follows the route of the southern most extremity of Wat's Dyke.) Go over the mill leat, past the mill ponds on the left, to reach the canal arm on your right and then continue over Croft Mill Lift Bridge. Turn left and follow the canal towpath east, past Bridge House.

The canal was built in 1795 to serve the local lime industry. It closed in 1936 after it had burst its banks and, as the railway had steadily been taking trade away, it was deemed uneconomic to repair. However, some sections were restored and reopened in 2003 for leisure use. On the left is a wildlife area where a pair of swans regularly nest. They can be seen with their cygnets on the canal in the spring.

On the right along this stretch are bullace trees - wild plums – that thrive in relatively undisturbed ground and old hedgerows, suggesting that this area has been relatively unchanged since the canal was built.

3. For refreshments, go through the gate on the right just before the next bridge and turn right to Canal Central Cafe and Post Office. Otherwise continue along the towpath under the bridge.

The field beyond the hedge on the right was called 'Canal Meadow' on the 1839 map and still looks much the same today as it did then. On the left was the 'Common Field', part of which is now used for housing. On the left, before the bridge is a high wall and hedge, beyond which can sometimes be glimpsed Llwyn Onn. The original frontage of this house faced south with lands on both sides of the canal, but when the canal bisected the property in 1795 the house was remodelled to turn the main entrance towards the road.

The Navigation Inn, Maesbury Marsh

Just before the bridge there is now a British Waterway's service block. Pennal Cottage and the land behind the service block was probably the original gatehouse for Llwyn Onn. From about the mid 19th century this was an industrial wharf with a large warehouse.

Go under Navigation Bridge, passing the Navigation Inn on the left.

The Navigation Inn was a pub before the canal was built, although the present name undoubtedly relates to the canal. A single storey warehouse was built next to the canal, probably in 1795, and this was extended upwards over the years and joined to the pub to make the present L-shaped building.

The first industrial area was just beyond the Navigation Inn. Here there were wharves for coal, timber, bricks etc, mainly for onward transportation to Oswestry. the barges also carried products from the 'bone manure works' whose chimney is still visible on the left.

Continue along the towpath to Park Mill Bridge. This area was mostly impenetrable marsh until the canal was built and the land drained.

4. To detour to St Winifred's Well.Go up the steps on the right-hand side of Park Mill Bridge. Turn right through a gate then half left to cross a stile by a gate in the far left-hand corner. Follow the right-hand field boundary to a stile then a double stile bridge over a brook, a tributary of the Rivers Morda, Vyrnwy and Severn. Follow the only path which leads to the pretty and atmospheric St Winifred's Well. (The area around St Winifred's Well can be very muddy with spillage from the well so care should be taken.)

St Winefride was a 7th century Welsh princess, sworn to a life of chastity. Reputedly she was miraculously brought back to life by her uncle, St. Beuno, after being decapitated by a spurned suitor as she

St Winifred's Well

ran to take refuge in church at Holywell in Flintshire. A spring gushed from where her head fell and this water had healing properties. A large well was built at the site to accommodate the numerous pilgrims who came seeking cures.

Winefride later settled at an abbey in Gwytherin, near Llanrwst, becoming abbess and remaining there until her death. In the 12th century monks from Shrewsbury Abbey dug up her remains from her grave and moved them to Shrewsbury, arguing that she was feeling neglected in Gwytherin. It was hoped that her bones would attract many pilgrims hoping for healing miracles and bring wealth to Shrewsbury Abbey. The story features in 'A Morbid Taste of Bones,' the first of the Brother Cadfael books by Ellis Peters, popularised in a TV series.

Legend has it that, in 1138, the monks carrying Winefride's remains rested at Woolston, and a spring bubbled forth from the spot where her coffin was put down, just as had happened in Holywell at the site of her murder. Stone bathing pools were built for the pilgrims who came to immerse themselves in the healing waters, that reputedly cured sore eyes, wounds, bruises and broken bones.

Holy wells are usually associated with a religious building but this one is unusual in that it is now covered by a late medieval half-timbered cottage that was originally used as a courthouse although this may have succeeded an earlier chapel.

5. Rejoin the canal towpath at Park Mill Bridge. Continue along the towpath under Red Bridge past the 3 sets of locks, known collectively as Aston Locks. Go under the new A5 Bridge then up the slope at the side of the Queen's Head Bridge. Turn left along the B5009 to return to the car park.

Ruabon Circular

Distance: 8km (5 miles)
Time: 2.5 - 3 hrs

A walk around the historic town of Ruabon along sections of both Wat's Dyke & Offa's Dyke and the opportunity to view an Iron Age hillfort.

Parking: At time of writing free car parking is available at Station Road but there is also parking in Ruabon centre.
Grid Ref: SJ300438; **Map:** OS Explorer 256.
Facilities: Shops and pubs in Ruabon.

The Walk

Ruabon is nowadays a peaceful small town but in the 18th and 19th century it was a thriving industrial centre as it sits on rich deposits of coal, iron, limestone and clay. The town grew rapidly during the Industrial Revolution as iron foundries and numerous coal mines opened. Some of the coal mines closed following flooding in 1846 but other pits flourished as drainage systems improved and the last local colliery continued working until 1968. However, Ruabon is perhaps best-known for the famous Ruabon brick and terracotta. This industry has outlasted all the others and Ruabon is now the only place in the UK still making quarry tiles.

1. From Ruabon station, walk back along Station Road and turn left into Bridge Street. Continue past the 'Roundhouse' (an early 18th century jail used to imprison drunks and

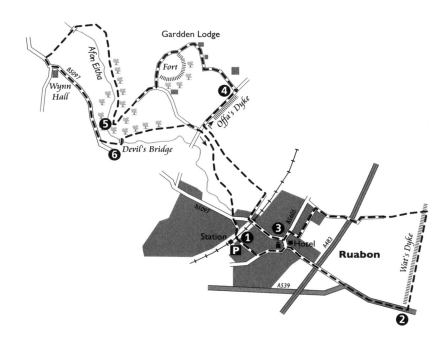

undesirables overnight). Just before the Wynnstay Arms, an old coach-house, turn right into Park Street and go past the stone workers cottages built by the Wynnstay Estate.

Wynnstay was originally known as Watstay, a reference to Wat's Dyke that runs through the park. Wynnstay was the main home of the Williams-Wynns, one of the richest and most powerful families in Wales during the 18th and 19th centuries. The entrance to Wynnstay Park is on the right. Ruabon was closely associated with the estate. Many of the older buildings were built by successive baronets and the church was lavishly endowed by the family.

Cross over the dual carriageway, ignoring the footpath on the left immediately after the bridge, and continuing ahead past Vicarage Fields to the crest of the hill.

The Roundhouse, Ruabon

2. Turn left through a kissing gate into a field and follow the footpath alongside a well preserved section of Wat's Dyke, with its deep ditch on the left. Continue alongside the dyke to the kissing gate at the far end of the field (ignore kissing gate halfway along field on left). Go through and turn left, then continue downhill and cross back over the dual carriageway via the footbridge joining Maes-y-Llan Road. Go past the school, then take the public footpath left just after Ruabon Village Hall, passing the bowling green. At the end of the children's play area turn right down a small alley then left onto New High Street.

3. Before reaching the Wynnstay Arms cross the road and turn right along Church Street passing the church on the left.

The St Mary 's Church was established by the Cistercian monks of Valle Crucis Abbey soon after 1272 but was extensively modified in the 18th and 19th centuries. Inside there is a 14th century fresco entitled, 'The Works of Mercy' and an exquisite Robert Adam font.

Beyond the church on the left is the old endowed school founded in 1618 and used as a school until 1858. Further on the right are the almshouses, which were built in 1711, a gift from the Reverend John Robinson.

Cross over the railway bridge and turn almost immediately right towards the cemetery. Keep to the right of the main arched entrance to go through a kissing gate. Follow the footpath along the edge of the cemetery where cow parsley and pink-flowered rosebay willow herb grow in abundance. Go through the next kissing gate and turn left following the cemetery boundary. Cross the stile and continue straight ahead into the next field with the hedge on your right. Go ahead to go through a gate, which leads to Tatham Farm.

Tatham Farm, originally two farms, takes its name from Richard Tatham who was tenant around 1784.

Almshouses, Ruabon

Bear right through the farmyard, then left passing the recent barn conversions to reach the road. Turn right and walk downhill along the road, which runs alongside Offa's Dyke, the bank on your right.

Offa's Dyke was constructed in the 8th century by Offa, King of Mercia. It is approximately 138 km (80 miles) long and provided a boundary between England and Wales. It remains the longest linear earthwork in Europe.

The land towards the end of this road was rich in clay. The discovery of vast quantities of this high quality Etruria Marl clay around Ruabon in the 19th century heralded the beginning of tile and terracotta production on a vast scale. By the turn of the century over 2000 people were employed in the industry, producing vast amounts of bricks, tiles and other terracotta products. The hard and shiny Ruabon red brick has been used for many local buildings and, due to its exceptional quality, it was also widely used for important buildings in industrial cities across Victorian Britain, including several universities. The collective name 'redbrick universities' refers to these Ruabon bricks - Liverpool University, built in 1892, is a fine example.

4. Turn left just before the Industrial Estate onto a lane. Walk steeply uphill along the lane whose verges are full of flowers in spring and summer, including herb robert, wild garlic, hart's tongue fern, foxglove and woody nightshade.

Follow the bend to the right past a chalet-type house. A little further on the left is the Ice-House and on the right is the site of Gardden Lodge.

Icehouses were a feature of 19th century estates. Built to store meat, these buildings were usually constructed with thick walls and often partly underground for extra insulation. The large bulk of ice collected in the winter would keep meat edible for up to a year. Gardden Lodge was the home of the High Sheriff of Denbighshire, Edward Rowland, in the early 19th century.

Chapel built of Ruabon brick

Carry on around the bend and past Pen-y-coed. Here the remains of the prehistoric hillfort come into view.

Gardden Fort possibly dates back to the early Iron Age, about 2500 years ago. Extending to four acres, and partly enclosed by a dry stone wall, it was defended by two banks and three ditches on the south side. The fort has never been fully excavated, but it probably housed a large community living in wooden roundhouses, until the Roman invasion of AD 55. It may have been occupied up to the 8th century.

In 1167 a battle was fought on this site between Owain Cyfeliog, Prince of Upper Powys, and the English and Normans. This battle was won by the Welsh and the poem 'Hirlas Eucin' was written to commemorate the event. 'Hirlas' is the name given to the long, blue horn, which is used for celebrations and can still be seen in ceremonies at the National Eisteddfod. This battle is also credited for the naming of the Afon Goch, which is reputed to have overflowed with the blood of the English - 'goch' being the Welsh word for red. This is one possible derivation of the name Ruabon, from Rhydd Avon, which means Reddish River.

Turn right by the semi-detached Ruabon brick houses; go past the stone cottage on the left to follow the path, which leads left into 'Rocky Woods'

Gardden Wood is known locally as 'Rocky Woods' because of the three old sandstone quarries, which supplied stone to North Wales, Lancashire and Cheshire until 1952.

Follow the marker posts past a sandstone quarry on the right then, where the path bears left, turn right and carry on for a few metres to turn left at a T-junction down a small slope. Keep going downhill to pass another quarry on the left. Continue on along a narrow ridge, with a chain mesh fence on the left, between the quarry and the river valley. Near the bottom go ahead to find a broad cart track and waymarker.

5. Turn right and follow the track through the wood keeping the river, Afon Eitha, on the left. Leave the wood by a large beech tree and continue ahead keeping the river and hedge on the left.

At the far end of the field cross a stile in a metal fence and go over an old embankment. Emerging from the trees bear half-left then down a slope to find a slightly indistinct path, which leads to a footbridge. Cross the bridge and continue ahead up the gentle slope to cross a stile by a metal gate. Continue along the track to the road, turning left then almost immediately left again to pass Wynn Hall on the right.

17th century Wynn Hall is named after the family who built it. In 1670 William Wynn was a commissioner named in the 1650 Act of Propagating the Gospel in Wales. He was a puritan and staunch supporter of Cromwell and Parliament during the Civil War between the Cavaliers, who supported the king, and Oliver Cromwell's Roundheads. He died in 1692 and was buried in the Dissenters Graveyard, Wrexham.

Continue along the B5097 road for 500m then turn left to descend down a bridletrack back into the woods. Turn left to cross the famous 'Devil's Bridge' over the river, a notorious spot for suicides in the 18th century.

6. At the end of the bridge turn right along the track, eventually passing some red brick cottages before reaching the road. Cross the road and go up the steps slightly to the right. Go through the kissing gate and walk along the top of the steep bank, near to the hedge. On the far side of this field follow the path, over the stile, along the boardwalk and through trees. Go through a gate and climb steps to the road then turn right.

Take the lane to the left of the Great Western pub, signed to the station, and follow it to the footbridge across the river.

Beside the waterfall look out for spring flowers, including bluebells and wild garlic, with its white flowers and distinctive pungent smell.

Go under the railway bridge and follow the path back to Station Road.

Rhosesmor Circular

Distance: 11.2km (7.0 miles)
Time: allow 3 - 3.5hrs

This circular walk explores **Moel y Gaer** Iron Age hillfort, from which there are magnificent views across the **Dee Estuary** and the **Clwydian Range**, then passes through **Rhosesmor** village then on across farmland and through woodland before following quiet country lanes back to **Rhosesmor.**

Parking: Viewpoint layby on B5123, Rhosesmor to Halkyn road, north of Rhos Helyg School.
Grid ref: SJ 209698. **Map:** OS Explorer 265.
Facilities: Shop & pubs in Rhosemor and Halkyn.

The Walk

1. From the layby turn left (when facing the road) and walk towards Rhosesmor. Just after passing Rhos Helyg School, cross the B5123 onto a gravel track, passing a small group of houses on the right. When the gravel track forks continue straight ahead to join a grassy path, which contours the lower slopes around Moel y Gaer.

(It is worth taking a short diversion to climb to the top of Moel y Gaer. Contour the lower slopes for about 400m then turn sharp right to follow a path up the hillside past the edge of a quarry. This leads to what was the main entrance to the hillfort crossing through a double set of earth banks and

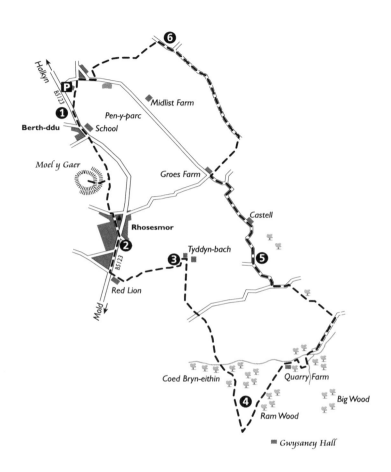

ditches. After enjoying the views return to where you left the path contouring the lower slopes).

Moel y Gaer, at a height of 303 metres, is the highest point on Halkyn Common. From its commanding position there are panoramic views to the west along the chain of hillforts on the Clwydian Range, and east and south across the Dee Estuary to the Wirral and Lancashire.

The earth banks and ditches encircling the summit are the remains of an Iron Age hillfort, built 2500 years ago. Within the fort remains of roundhouses were found, plus three small rectangular buildings that were probably storehouses or granaries, raised off the ground to protect food from vermin.

It is said that in 1403, Hywel Gwynedd set up a camp on the hill during his support of Owain Glyndwr's revolt.The hilltop was also used during the Napoleonic wars when a fire beacon was built in 1814 to warn of French invasion from the sea.

Continue towards Rhosesmor joining a gravel track by Rock Cottage. At the road junction continue ahead, passing St Paul's Church on the left, to reach a cross roads with a phone box opposite.

The area now known as Rhosesmor was little more than a scattered farming hamlet, known as Caerfallwch, until the lead mining boom of the 19th century. The village grew rapidly as miners moved into the area and St Paul's Church, which was consecrated on 21 April 1876, was built to serve the growing population.

Caer translates as fort and probably refers to the hillfort. Afallwch or Afallach may have been an early Welsh leader, hence Caerfallwch means 'Afallach's fort'. There may even be a link with King Arthur. Arthur's final resting place is known to most as Avalon, but Welsh texts record the name as Afallwch so Moel y Gaer is one of the many places that could claim to be the burial site of King Arthur!

2. Cross the main road then turn right and continue through Rhosesmor. Just before the 17th century Red Lion pub turn left onto the marked track. Walk along the track past a garage workshop and go over a stile/gate by house. Follow the left-hand field boundary down to cross a stile then go through the gate opposite. Turn right and follow the right-hand hedgerow down the field to a gate. Go through the gate and continue ahead joining a farm track. Go around a left-hand

View of the Clwydian Range from Moel y Gaer

bend then look for footpath finger post on the right-hand side opposite the farm. There is a stone stile alongside the fingerpost. Ignore this stile and, instead, go through the metal gate on the right into the field (away from the farm).

3. Walk along left-hand hedgerow to cross an indistinct stile in the field corner. Continue with the field boundary on the left over 4 stiles to reach a tarmac lane. Cross the lane and over a stile into a field opposite then continue ahead with hedge on the right to reach another stile. Cross this stile and continue, intitially keeping the hedge on the left. When the hedge turns sharp left continue straight across the field to a stile on the opposite boundary. Cross stile and walk downhill through a group of trees in the field. At the bottom cross a small wooden sleeper bridge and stile into woodland. Follow the path uphill to a private track. Turn left along track for 20m then turn right and climb steeply uphill through the woods (path is not easy to follow) to cross a stile at the top into a field. Bear half-right across the field to go over a stile by a gate. Walk across the right-hand corner of the next field to cross a hidden stile to the left of a gateway. Walk diagonally left across a large field to opposite field corner, which is down in a dip, passing a small derelict barn. Turn left onto a track, walking uphill with the brick wall of Gwasaney Estate on the right.

4. Go though a kissing gate and follow the track through woodland to reach a gate/stile. Cross stile and walk along the right-hand field boundary to end of the field. Turn right over two stiles / gates to join the track by Quarry Farm. Follow this track down a steep hill for about 1 km. Turn left over a concealed stile, 100m before the tarmac road, and follow the left-hand hedge then cross a stile into the next field. Pass a wood on the right and continue across field to cross a stile onto tarmac road. Turn left along road.

5. After 150m turn right uphill. Follow this lane for approximately 250m then fork right at the next junction. Continue on lane for approximately 1km, passing Castell on the left. Turn left at junction and continue towards Groes Farm. Just before the farm go right over the stone stile and follow the waymarked path down the slope to a gate. Continue ahead following the line of telegraph poles. Cross two adjacent stiles then a third to the left of a small pond, over a small wooden bridge to cross a final stile onto a grassy track (Note: this track can be very muddy.) Turn left and follow the track along the edge of a wood to a junction with a tarmac lane

The track and lane are part of the old coach road, which ran from Chester to Holywell via Halkyn, until replaced by the original A55 built in 1826-7.

Continue ahead along the road for 150m then turn left up a concrete track towards Midlist Farm.

Midlist Farm have been rearing water buffalo since 1998 when fifty were imported from Romania. Water buffalo are originally from Asia

where they are still used as draught animals as well as for meat and milk. Nowadays water buffalo can also be found in Europe notably in Italy, where they are milked to make the world famous mozzarella cheese. They are placid animals that make better use of poorer quality feed than cattle. Mature grass can be harvested late in the season to make a drier more coarse winter feed, which suits their digestive system.

6. Follow this track for 300m. Where it turns left, leave the concrete track and bear right uphill on a grass path with a small copse on the right to reach a stile. Cross this stile and follow the telegraph pole markers across the field to a metal stile. Cross the stile and follow the right-hand field boundary over 2 further metal stiles then turn left towards a pond to reach a road. Turn right up the road and, at the converted chapel on the right, take the track opposite on the left to return to the layby at the beginning of the walk.

Water buffalo at Midlist Farm

Holywell Circular

Distance: 6.0 km (3.7 miles)
Time: allow 1.5 - 2 hrs

A pleasant short walk from Holywell crossing Wat's Dyke then continuing with stunning views over the Dee Estuary, before returning along quiet country lanes to Holywell.

Parking: Car park opposite Lidl or Bank Place car park, Holywell.
Grid ref: SJ 188759; **Map:** OS Explorer 265.
Facilities: Shops & pubs in Holywell.

The Walk

1. From the small car park opposite Lidl walk towards Lidl supermarket. Cross over Pen-y-maes Road, turn left then almost immediately right into Rose Hill. Walk down Rose Hill to the end and cross over the A5026 Bagillt Road to some steps, which lead down to a minor road. Bear right downhill to cross over a stream. Continue briefly uphill then turn right at the footpath sign and kissing gate into Llwybr-y-bi woods.

It is difficult to translate Llwybr-y-bi into English, but one possible derivation is 'path of the magpie'.

2. Follow the waymarked path initially towards the stream then to the steps on your left. Climb these and turn right along the path, which runs parallel to the stream, Nant-y-Fflint. The path then gradually descends back towards the stream before joining another steep, but graded path, on the left uphill. This

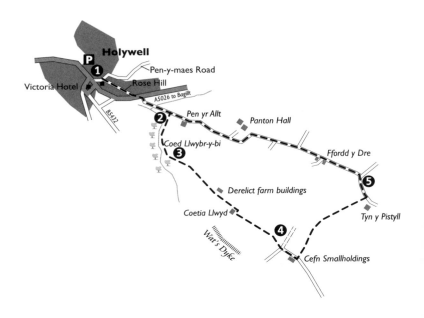

part of the route crosses the line of Wat's Dyke, visible as a steep bank, before going over a stile into a large field.

3. Go ahead along the left-hand field edge and over a stile in the far corner. Continue along the left-hand edge of the next field to cross a stile in the corner.

There are stunning views over the Dee Estuary to the Wirral, Hilbre Island and, on a clear day, to Liverpool, with its distinctive cathedral, and on up the Lancashire coast.

Continue ahead past derelict, red-brick, farm buildings, past a waymarked stile on the left and on along the left-hand field edge to cross two stiles at the bottom of the garden of Coetia-Llwyd. After the second stile, at a waymarked path junction, turn right over a stile then immediately left to follow the left-hand field edge. Cross over a stile in the far corner, and on across the middle of the next field to cross a stile in the boundary ahead by a large tree.

Looking back towards Holywell a converted 18th century windmill is visible. Local farmers used to bring their grain to be ground at the mill.

Now go half-right to join and follow a hedge. Then cross a stile onto a track/lane, signed National Cycle Trail No. 5.

4. Continue ahead up the tarmac lane towards the green barn. Take the footpath over the stile on the left, opposite the entrance to Cefn Smallholdings. Go down the right-hand field edge, through a gateway in the field corner, then go down the left-hand partial boundary of the next field to a footpath post then cross a narrow stream and stile beyond. Go ahead along the left-hand hedge boundary - now enjoying new views east to the Dee Bridge at Flint, and, in the distance, Beeston Castle and the Peckforton Hills in Cheshire. When it bends left, continue down the field aiming half-right for a hedge corner to the left of large farm outbuildings. Cross a stile by a gate in a kink in the boundary ahead. Follow the boundary on the left, over two stiles on the left of the barn, then drop down through a gap in the boundary ahead onto a lane. Follow it left. At a junction by a house, turn left onto Old Bagillt Road and follow this quiet country lane that was once the main route between Holywell, Bagillt and Flint.

Look out for bees along this section in the verge flowers during the late spring and summer. There are seven major species of bumble bee in Britain, their stripes or bands varying with white, yellow, orange, gold and black colouration. Their annual colonies, formed in nests of grass and moss, often inhabit well-drained earth banks. They produce about 100 workers, which collect nectar and pollen to rear the young. Later in the year the queen lays eggs, which produce males and females. After pairing the females hibernate for winter and form new colonies in spring.

View across the Dee Estuary

5. Pass Ffordd y Dre Farm (Town Road Farm) on your left and then a small lane on the right to Tyn Twll Farm. The lane then bends left then right. Pass the drive to Panton Hall on the right. Continue past a cottage (Pen yr Allt) on your left to go down hill to the kissing gate that you went through on your way out. Retrace your steps back to the car park crossing the A5026, and then along the road opposite (Rose Hill) back into Holywell Centre.

About the author

Pete Lewis was brought up in Ewloe and spent his formative years exploring the mountains and coast of North Wales. He is an aeronautical engineer by training who worked for many years at British Aerospace and later as a management consultant. His early love of the countryside and walking remained with him throughout this time and he also developed a great interest in local history. In 2005 he co-wrote 'Rural Walks in Flintshire' for Flintshire Countryside Service and has researched walks for several other publications. He hopes that this book will stimulate interest in the history of Wat's Dyke.